Rejoicing in the Year

Services celebrating the Church's seasons

David Adam

kevin mayhew

kevin
mayhew

First published in Great Britain in 2011 by Kevin Mayhew Ltd
Buxhall, Stowmarket, Suffolk, IP14 3BW
Tel: +44 (0) 1449 737978 Fax: +44 (0) 1449 737834
E-mail: info@kevinmayhewltd.com

www.kevinmayhew.com

9 8 7 6 5 4 3 2 1 0

ISBN 978 1 84867 368 7
Catalogue No. 1501271

Cover design by Rob Mortonson

Edited and typeset by Free Range Book Design & Production Limited

Printed and bound in Great Britain

Contents

About the author 7
Introduction 9

Morning and evening prayer 15
Morning prayer 1 16
Morning prayer 2 18
Morning prayer 3 20
Morning prayer 4 22

Advent 25
Advent 1
People of faith 26
Abraham and God's faithful people 31
Advent 2
People of Vision 34
Isaiah and Visionaries 39
Advent 3
People immersed in God 42
John the Baptist 47
Advent 4
People in love with God 50
The Blessed Virgin Mary 55

Title of the Christ
O Sapientia – The Wisdom of God: *17 December* 58
O Adonai – The Lord of lords: *18 December* 61
O Radix Jesse – Root of Jesse: *19 December* 64
O Clavis David – The Key of David: *20 December* 67
O Oriens – Christ the Morning Star: *21 December* 70
O Rex Gentium – King of the nations: *22 December* 73
O Emmanuel – God with us: *23 December* 76

Christmas 79
Carol service 80
The Christmas story 86
Christmas Eve 92
Christmas Day 95

The Epiphany 97
The Epiphany 98
The wise men 104
The Baptism of our Lord 107
Immersed in God 110
Celebrating the water made wine 116
The transforming power of Christ 121
The mission of the Church 125
Working with Christ 127

Candlemas 129
The Lord is my light 130
The presentation of Christ in the Temple 133

Lent 139
Ash Wednesday 140
Lent 1 – Temptations 145
Lent 2 – The battle against evil 150
Lent 3 – Suffering 155
Lent 4 – Mothering Sunday 160
Lent 5 – Passion 165
Palm Sunday 170
Good Friday
The Way of the Cross 175

Easter	193
Easter Vigil	194
Easter Day	207
Easter Garden	209
Easter 2	
The risen Lord and Mary	221
Rejoice in the Lord	226
Easter 3	
The risen Lord and ten disciples	229
The peace of the risen Lord	234
Easter 4	
The risen Lord and Thomas	237
The risen Lord comes to our doubts	242
Easter 5	
The risen Lord, Cleopas and companion	245
The risen Lord on the road to Emmaus	250
Easter 6	
The risen Lord on the shore	253
The risen Lord is always with us	258
Ascension Day	262
The risen and ascended Lord	269
The Sunday after the Ascension	271
The risen and ascended Christ	276
Pentecost	279
Holy Spirit, inspire us	284
Trinity	287
Transfiguration	290
All Saints	292

Remembrance Day 294

Other Occasions 303
Birth 304
Journeying 306
Loved ones leaving 309
In times of darkness 311
A light for someone 313
For the departed 315

Acknowledgements 319

About the author

David Adam was the Vicar of Lindisfarne, off the Northumbrian coast, for thirteen years until he retired in March 2003. His work involved ministering to thousands of pilgrims and other visitors. He is the author of many inspiring books on spirituality and prayer, and his Celtic writings have rekindled a keen interest in our Christian heritage.

Other books by David Adam:

1000 Prayers for Public Worship
A Prayer a Day for Lent
A Prayer a Day from Advent to Epiphany
Candle Prayers
Candles in the Dark
Complete Common Worship Sermon Illustrations
Daily Prayer
Growing in Awareness
Growing in Grace
Growing in the Light
Knowing and Growing
Looking and Longing
Prayers for Anglicans
Prayers of Intercession for Common Worship
Rejoicing in Newness of Life
Searchlights, Years A, B and C
The Complete Themed Intercessions
The Echo of God
The Great 'I Am'
The Way of the Cross
Themed Sermon Illustrations
Walking into the Light
Waters of Life Series
Welcoming the Light

Introduction

> For everything there is a season, and a time for every matter under heaven.
>
> *Ecclesiastes 3:1*

We live in a world of rhythms and seasons. Each day has its sunrise and sunset; its day and its night. Each year has its spring, summer, autumn and winter. There are times for planting and times for harvesting; times of pruning and times of growing; there are times for activity and times for rest. We learn to adjust with the seasons. Some adjustments are natural and others are patterns that we have created. We measure our waking day with activity, rest and play, creating spaces to stop and eat to replenish energy levels. Like the tides, our heart has its own rhythm governed by diastole and systole – the filling and emptying of the heart of blood – periods where the heart is relaxing and where it is under pressure, both are necessary to a healthy rhythm. Our bodies have complex rhythms that we need to work with.

In the twenty first century many of the rhythms have been overlaid by our way of living. By artificial light we can work at night. If we live in a city we are not so geared to the seasons. Food is grown throughout the year in heated greenhouses and imported from abroad. We can buy the fruit we want all the year around. So we no longer feel attached to seedtime and harvest. The danger is that we get out of touch with the rhythmic patterns of ourselves and the world around us. By working with the seasons we can get so much more out of life.

The Church has built two major seasons into the year to help us in our growth and learning. Both of these seasons are related to the life of Jesus. The first season is concerned with the coming of the promised Saviour. This is the Incarnation Season, beginning with the four Sundays before Christmas, called Advent because they concentrate on the coming of the promised Christ. The Incarnation Season continues with Christmas and the birth of Jesus. This is followed by the Epiphany and the revelation of Jesus to the world. The Incarnation Season ends on 2 February when we celebrate the Presentation of Christ in the Temple, often known as 'Candlemas'.

There is now a short gap which varies in length according to the date of Easter. The second season is the Resurrection Season which is concerned with the death and resurrection of Jesus. It begins on Ash Wednesday and goes through to Pentecost. Ash Wednesday and the Lent Season are a time of preparation for Easter, a time of developing our faith and looking at our priorities in relationship to God. Holy Week is the time leading up to the crucifixion, which is remembered on Good Friday. Easter is a great time of rejoicing for it is a time to celebrate the resurrection and the gift of eternal life. This continues until Pentecost, where we remember the coming of the Spirit.

These two seasons are known as the Temporale. The rest of the year is known as Ordinary Time, a time which is used to reflect on the teaching and daily life of Jesus. Into the year is added the Sanctorale, which are the saints' days when we are given the opportunity to learn from, and be inspired by, the lives of faithful men and women throughout the ages.

This book is primarily concerned with the Church's two major seasons and also to give us the opportunity for Morning and Evening Prayer. The aim is to give a rhythm to the year that is based on the Church's teaching and to help us focus on the saving acts of our Lord. We need to hear again and again the wonderful events that are for us and for our salvation. Each time, if we keep ourselves open, the words and their reality should enter deeper into our own being and make us more and more aware of the love of God. We shall never fully comprehend the mystery of the life, death and resurrection of Christ. We can never say we fully understand what is said. But we can allow the presence and love of God to be wrapped around us each time we hear the Good News, allowing the reality of what is said enter deeper into our lives. Just as a nail cannot be driven home by one blow of the hammer we do not learn the faith by a single hearing or action. Throughout our lives we have the opportunity to grow in awareness and in the love of God. I pray that this book may help you in that journey.

Although these services are designed for use with others, and as services in church, all that is contained within this book can be used in various ways.

At home for personal or family devotions.
At any time of a family get together or before a meal.
As a means of affirming the presence
and that we are in God's hands.

At the start of a study group or meeting.
At the beginning of a confirmation class.
At the lighting of the candles before a service.
As a meditation on the saving works of God.

To get the best out of any of these services it is important not to rush the occasion but to savour it. As a starting point it is necessary to fix a place and a time for our prayers. Without this we are in danger of having 'no time' and no place to pray. For many people it has been beneficial to light a candle to remind them of God's presence whenever they come to pray. You might like to choose a special candle and holder for this purpose.

Candle-lighting is an act of faith. It is affirming our belief that God is here with us; that God loves us and gives himself to us. Candle-lighting does not make God come to us, for God is already with us. It helps to open our hearts and minds to his coming. Candle-lighting does not make God do things – that would be magic! God is already active in our lives and through candle-lighting we seek to focus on that reality.

In the Incarnation Season, from its beginning in Advent to its end on Candlemas, I have suggested that you light a candle each time. In the same way I have suggested using a lighted candle to remind us of the light and love revealed in the presence of the risen Lord from Easter Day until Pentecost. On these occasions it is a good idea to begin in the dark. If the room is not dark, close your eyes. Much of our life is spent in the dark and this is a symbol of our life without God, even though God is there in our darkness. You might like to affirm in the dark – the 'Lord is here' – or use some positive words about the presence and power of God.

Now welcome the light, the light of God, into your life and your heart. You may like to give thanks for Jesus who is the Light of the world.

Use some words of Scripture, a poem or a reading at this point to focus on why you have lit the candle at this time.

If you have any special intention quietly lay this before God. During this time focus on the light and know that the light of God is with you and within you.

Relax in the light of God, concentrate on the light and allow God's light into your life. Let his light shine in your heart and in your eyes.

Seek to know that the light of God is with us all, envisage that the light surrounds each of your loved ones and for all whom you want to pray for. Know that his presence is with them and his love is all about them. Pray that God's light may shine through you and reveal his light to others, that you may give out the light of God when the world around is in darkness. Seek God's blessing of light

Finally put the candle out. (Remember leaving untended candles can be dangerous). At this point ask that you may take the light with you in your heart and mind.

For the Advent season you may like to have special candles. The Advent candles are normally held together in an Advent wreath. To make an Advent wreath to hold the candles of Advent and Christmas is quite simple. Firstly, obtain a circle of oasis from a florists and add greenery to it (this reminds us that we are dealing with eternal events). Now add four candles, some people like to use purple candles to say it is Advent. In the centre of the circle add one larger white candle to represent Christ's arrival, 'God with us'. Advent is at the darkest time of the year, so it is good to bring a little light to it. The first week we will light one candle, the second two, by Christmas we will have lit all five. Then we will continue to light the five each week until Candlemas. We will need to replace any burnt out candles with new ones. The burnt out candles are symbols of those who have given their life to Christ and in the renewing of them we should offer our life to God. To make a simpler wreath use tea lights on a tea plate with four around the outside and one in the centre, again replacing any that burn out. You can add a little greenery if you so wish.

In the same way you can have a special candle for the Easter Season. Easter candles can be bought from any church suppliers, or you can buy a transfer for a few pence and add it to a candle of your choice. However, it is good for a family to make the Easter candle at home. If possible use a large and chunky candle because it will be lit for fifty days, from Easter Day to Pentecost, although from Ascension Day you may want the candle to look a little different. On the candle inscribe a cross. Do not do this too high up or it will burn away too soon. At the head of the cross write the first letter of the Greek alphabet alpha (**A**) and the last letter at the foot of the cross Omega (**Ω**). You may want to inscribe the date below the Omega. This reminds us that our Lord said: 'I am the Alpha and the Omega, the First and the Last, the Beginning and the End'. Now using five studs, or brass drawing pins, you could add the wounds of Christ: one at the head of the cross for the crown of thorns; two on the arms of the cross for the nails that held his hands; one for the nail that held his feet; and one for the lance that pierced his side. Your Easter candle should look like this.

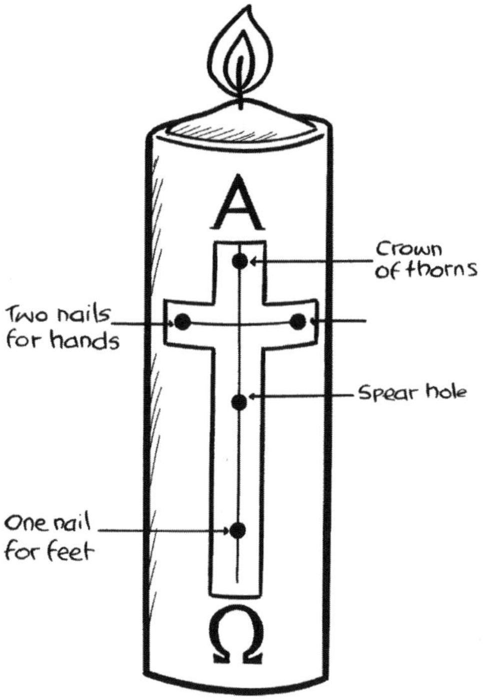

If you prefer, a simple candle or tea light can be used. The important thing is to celebrate the triumph of our Lord over darkness and death, to rejoice that in him, the Light of the World, life is eternal.

At all times, the candle is there to remind you of the power, the peace and above all the presence of our God. In all our worship we affirm that God is always with us, he never leaves us: in his love he enfolds us. Rejoice for the Lord is here and his presence is with us.

Morning and Evening prayer

Morning prayer 1

Begin in the dark. If the room is not dark, close your eyes. In the dark affirm the presence of God.

Welcome the light

By the tender mercy of our God,
the dawn from on high will break upon us,
to give light to those who sit in darkness,
and in the shadow of death,
to guide our feet into the way of peace.
Luke 1:78, 79

The Lord is here:
his spirit is with us

As we rejoice in the gift of this new day, may the light of your presence set our hearts on fire with love for you.
Common Worship, Morning Prayer

O God, Creator of light,
at the rising of your sun this morning,
let the greatest of all lights, your love,
rise like the sun within our hearts.
The Armenian Apostolic Church

Candle-lighting

Our God is the Light of the World:
a light that no darkness can quench.

The Light of Christ:
thanks be to God.

Light the candle.

Blessed are you, O Lord our God,
you are our light and salvation:
yours is the power, the glory, the splendour and the majesty,
now and always.
Open our ears to your call,
open our eyes to your light,
open our hearts to your love
that we may live to your praise and glory, now and always,
Father, Son and Holy Spirit.
Blessed be God for ever.

Special intention – in the light of God

We bring before you, O Lord,
the troubles and dangers of peoples and nations:
the sighing of prisoners and captives,
the sorrows of the bereaved,
the needs of strangers,
the helplessness of the weak,
the despondency of the weary,
the failing powers of the aged.
Upon all let your love and light shine,
for the sake of Christ the Light of the World.
Amen.

Adapted from a prayer of St Anselm c.1033–1109

Closing prayer

Light of Jesus surround us.
Light of Jesus guide us.
Light of Jesus be within us.
Light of Jesus protect us.
Light of Jesus enfold us.
Light of Jesus transform us,
that we may be children of the Light
and walk in your Light.

Stay for a while rejoicing in the light of Christ.

Extinguish candle.

Morning prayer 2

Begin in the dark. If the room is not dark, close your eyes.

Welcome the light

Arise, shine; for your light is come, and the glory of the Lord is risen upon you. For darkness shall cover the earth, and thick darkness the peoples: but the glory of the Lord will rise upon you, and his glory will appear over you.

Isaiah 60:1, 2

We are in the light and love of the Lord:
Glory to the Father, Son and Holy Spirit.

O God, you brought us from the rest of night
to the light of this new day.
Bring us from the light this day
to the guiding light of eternity.

Traditional

Candle-lighting

Light of God shine upon us:
and scatter the darkness from within us and about us.

Light the candle.

Blessed are you Lord our God for you have called us out of darkness to be children of Light. The bright light of your presence scatters the darkness within us and is a lantern to our paths. Bless this light that it may remind us of your presence among us and of your love; through Christ our Lord.
Amen.

Light of God shining in our lives and throughout the world:
may we see and reflect the radiance of your glory.

Hymn
Christ, whose glory fills the skies

Special intention – in the light of God

Help us Lord:
to live in your light,
to act in your might,
to think in your wisdom,
to walk in your kingdom,
to abide in your love;
your presence to prove.
Amen.

Closing prayer

You encircle us, O God.
you surround us with your love.
you offer to us your light.
you enfold us in your peace.
you are with us this day and always.
you encircle us, O God.

Stay for a while rejoicing in the light of Christ.

Extinguish candle.

Evening prayer 1

Begin in the dark. If the room is not dark, close your eyes.

Welcome the light

The Lord, my God, lights up my darkness.
Psalm 18:28

Come, my Lord, my Light, my Way;
come, my lantern night and day;
come my healer, make me whole;
come my Saviour protect my soul;
come my King, enter my heart;
come Prince of Peace and never depart.
Come my King, enter my heart;
come Prince of Peace and never depart.

Candle-lighting

Our God is the Light of the World:
a light that no darkness can quench.

The Light of Christ:
thanks be to God.

Light the candle.

Blessed are you Lord God, Creator of all things,
you give life and light to the world.
As we light this candle to disperse the darkness
may the light of your love burn within our hearts.
Blessed are you Father, Son and Holy Spirit.

Reading

The Lord is my light and my salvation; whom shall I fear?
The Lord is my light and my salvation.

The Lord is the stronghold of my life; of whom shall I be afraid?
The Lord is my light and my salvation.

Glory be to the Father, and to the Son, and to the Holy Spirit.
The Lord is my light and my salvation.

Psalm 27:1, 2

Special intention – in the light of God

Pray for all whom you have met this day,
those you have worked with,
those you live with
and all who need your prayers.

Watch, thou dear Lord,
with those who wake, or watch, or weep tonight,
and give your angels charge over those who sleep.
Tend your sick ones, Lord Christ,
rest your weary ones,
bless your dying ones,
soothe your suffering ones,
pity your afflicted ones,
shield your joyous ones.
I ask all this for your love's sake.

St Augustine of Hippo 354–430

Closing prayer

God in the night,
God at my right,
God all the day,
God with me stay,
God in my heart
never depart.
God with thy might
keep us in light
through this dark night.

Extinguish candle.

Evening prayer 2

Begin in the dark. If the room is not dark, close your eyes.

Welcome the light

The presence, the power and the protection of God are with us and about us. We are in the Light of the Father, the Son and the Holy Spirit.

Candle-lighting

Our God is the Light of the World:
a light that no darkness can quench.

The Light of Christ:
thanks be to God.

Light the candle.

Blessed are you, Lord our God, you give us life and you continually renew and refresh us with your presence and your love. You are the strength of the weak and the light to all who walk in darkness.
Blessed are you Father, Son and Holy Spirit.

I come in weakness to the power of God.
God is my salvation; I will trust and not be afraid, for the Lord is my strength and my might; and has become my salvation.

Isaiah 12:2

I come in darkness to the light of God.
God is my salvation; I will trust and not be afraid, for the Lord is my strength and my might; and has become my salvation.

I come in fear to the peace of God.
God is my salvation; I will trust and not be afraid, for the Lord is my strength and my might; and has become my salvation.

I come with troubles to the healing of God.
God is my salvation; I will trust and not be afraid, for the Lord is my strength and my might; and has become my salvation.

I come in need to the love of God.
God is my salvation; I will trust and not be afraid, for the Lord is my strength and my might; and has become my salvation.

Hymn
O gracious light, Lord Jesus Christ

Special intention – in the light of God

Eternal Light, shine in our hearts:
Eternal Goodness, deliver us from evil;
Eternal Power, be our support;
Eternal Wisdom, scatter the darkness of our ignorance;
Eternal Pity, have mercy upon us;
that with all our heart and mind and soul and strength
we may seek your face
and be brought by your infinite mercy
to your Holy Presence;
through Jesus Christ our Lord.
Amen.

Alcuin of York 735–804

Closing prayer

Holy God, Holy and Strong One,
conquer the darkness within us and about us:
let your blessing rest upon us,
upon our homes and our loved ones,
that we may abide in your peace,
in your presence and in your light,
now and for evermore.
Amen.

Extinguish candle.

Advent

Advent 1
People of faith

Affirmation of God's presence

Affirmation

Advent is a time when we rejoice in the coming of Christ into our lives, that he came at Christmas, and that he comes again to be our Lord and King. Advent celebrates that our God comes to us again and again.

Today is the First Sunday in Advent, when we remember our ancestors in the faith and give thanks to God for all of his faithful people.

Invitation to worship

With all the faithful we rejoice in the presence, in the peace and in the power of God, Father, Son and Holy Spirit. **Amen.**

The Lord is here.
His Spirit is with us.

Hymn

Hark the glad sound! the Saviour comes

Silence

Candle-lighting

On the First Sunday in Advent we light one candle to say with all faithful people:

The Lord comes to us.
He abides with us.

When our lives are darkened it is necessary to celebrate the presence that comes to us and the light that is given to us.

The lighting of the Advent candle.

Jesus Christ is the Light of the World:
eternal light shine in our hearts.

When this world is as dark as night,
you are the one we call the Light.
Come, Lord Jesus.

When we are tempted to go astray,
you are the one we call the Way.
Come, Lord Jesus.

When the storms of life increase,
you are the one we call our Peace.
Come, Lord Jesus.

When troubles to our lives bring harm,
you are the one who brings us calm.
Come, Lord Jesus.

Blessed are you Lord our God, for you have called us out of darkness into your glorious light. We thank you for all our ancestors in the faith, for Abraham and Sarah, Isaac and Rebekah, Jacob and Rachel, for all who have passed on the faith to us. You are their God and our God, their Father and our Father. Help us to know that as you came to them you come to us.
Blessed be God for ever.

Silence

Ministry of the Word

Reading
Hebrews 11:6, 8–10, 23–27

Hymn
Lord of our life, and God of our salvation

The Gospel
Matthew 8:5–13

Sermon

Silence

Hymn
Have faith in God, my heart

Response

Creed

Confession

Thanksgiving
Praise and thanks to you, O God, for you have created us out of your love and for your love. You give us the opportunity to know you and to serve you. We give you thanks for all who have revealed your friendship in their lives. We thank you for our ancestors in the faith to whom you spoke as a friend. We rejoice that you have called us to be part of this household of faith, through Christ our Lord. **Amen.**

Intercessions
Blessed are you Lord our God for you are an ever-present help in our troubles, you are our strength and our salvation. We come before you in faith and seek your love.

We thank you for the Church throughout the world and for all who have kept faith in you. We ask your blessing upon all who are being persecuted for their faith, all who are being scorned or rejected because of their beliefs. We ask you to give new courage and hope to those who have lost faith and all who walk in darkness.
God of faith,
increase our love and trust in you.

We give thanks for the land in which we live and we ask your blessing upon all who are leaders in government and in society. May they be people of vision and committed to justice. We ask your blessing upon any who are suffering from disasters, from flood or famine and all who are uncertain of their future.
God of faith,
increase our love and trust in you.

We thank you for all the love we have received and we ask you to protect and guide all our friends and loved ones. Bless our homes and our families and enfold them in your love. We pray especially today for any who are suffering from the breakdown of family life or from broken relationships and all who have lost faith in others.
God of faith,
increase our love and trust in you.

We thank you for our well-being and we remember before you all who are ill or suffering, all who are finding life overwhelming and all who cannot cope. We pray especially for those who feel no one cares and are lonely.
God of faith,
increase our love and trust in you.

We join our prayers with all the faithful who have gone before and put our hope and trust in you.
Merciful Father,
accept these prayers for the sake of your Son, our Saviour Jesus Christ. Amen.

Collect

Almighty God, give us grace to cast away the works of darkness
and to put on the armour of light
now in the time of this mortal life,
in which your Son Jesus Christ came to visit us in great humility;
that on the last day
when he shall come again in his glorious majesty
to judge the living and the dead,
we may rise to the life immortal;

through him who is alive and reigns with you,
in the unity of the Holy Spirit,
one God, now and for ever.
Amen.

Common Worship Collect for Advent 1

The Lord's Prayer

Silence

Hymn
Thou didst leave thy throne

Blessing

God the Father
give you grace to know him and to love him;
Christ the Son grant you an awareness of his saving power;
the Holy Spirit guide you in the way of faithfulness and truth;
and the blessing of God Almighty,
the Father, the Son and the Holy Spirit
be upon you and your loved ones this day and for always.
Amen.

Advent 1
Abraham and God's faithful people

Advent is a time when we rejoice in the coming of Christ into our lives, that he came at Christmas, and that he comes again to be our Lord and King. Advent celebrates that our God comes to us again and again.

Begin in the dark. If the room is not dark, close your eyes.

Welcome the light

The people who walked in darkness have seen a great light; they who lived in a land of deep darkness, on them the light has shined.

Isaiah 9:2

Candle-lighting

On the first Sunday in Advent we light one candle to say with all faithful people:

The Lord comes to us.
He abides with us.

When our lives are darkened it is necessary to celebrate God's presence that comes to us and the light that God gives us.

Light one Advent candle.

Jesus Christ is the Light of the World:
Eternal Light, shine in our hearts.

Blessed are you, Lord our God, for you have called us out of darkness to be children of Light. The bright light of your presence scatters the it may remind us of your presence among us and your love towards us; through Christ our Lord.
Amen.

Reading
Genesis 18:1–15

Hymn
The God of Abraham praise *(third verse)*

Special intention – in the light of God

When this world is as dark as night,
you are the one we call the Light.
Come, Lord Jesus.

When we are tempted to go astray,
you are the one we call the Way.
Come, Lord Jesus.

When the storms of life increase,
you are the one we call our Peace.
Come, Lord Jesus.

When troubles to our lives bring harm,
you are the one who brings us calm.
Come, Lord Jesus.

Almighty God, give us grace to cast away the works of darkness and to put on the armour of light, now in the time of this mortal life, in which your Son Jesus Christ came to us in great humility; so that on the last day, when he shall come again in His glorious majesty to judge the living and the dead, we may rise to the life immortal; through Him who is alive and reigns with you and the Holy Spirit, one God, now and for ever. **Amen.**

Common Worship Collect for Advent 1

Closing prayer

Lord of Life, of Light, of Love,
come that I may fully live;
come that I may walk in the light;
come that I may burn with your love.
Come Lord this day, I welcome you.

Extinguish candle.

Advent 2
People of vision

Affirmation of God's presence

Affirmation

Advent is a time when we rejoice in the coming of Christ into our lives, that he came at Christmas, and that he comes again to be our Lord and King. Advent celebrates that our God comes to us again and again. Today is the Second Sunday in Advent when we remember the prophets and give thanks for all people of vision.

Invitation to worship

With all the prophets and people of vision we rejoice in the grace and goodness of God, Father, Son and Holy Spirit. **Amen.**

The Lord is here.
His Spirit is with us.

Hymn

Be thou my vision, O Lord of my heart

Silence

Candle-lighting

On the Second Sunday in Advent we light two candles, one for all of God's faithful people and one for men and women of vision.

When our lives are darkened it is necessary to celebrate the presence that comes to us and the vision that is given to us.

The Lord comes to us
He abides with us.

The lighting of the two Advent candles.

Jesus Christ is the Light of the World:
eternal light, shine in our hearts.

Lord, open our eyes to your presence.
Come, Lord of light.

Lord, open our ears to your call.
Come, Lord of light.

Lord, open our hearts to your love.
Come, Lord of light.

Lord, open our lives to your guiding.
Come, Lord of light.

Blessed are you Lord God for you open the eyes of the blind. You gave vision and insight to the prophets. We thank you for Amos and Hosea, for Isaiah, Jeremiah and Ezekiel and all the prophets, and for all people who have extended our awareness through their vision. You are their God and our God, their Father and our Father. Help us to know that as you came to them you come to us.
Blessed be God for ever.

Silence

Ministry of the Word

Reading
Isaiah 9:2, 3, 6, 7

Hymn
Come, thou long-expected Jesus

The Gospel
Luke 10:23, 24

Sermon

Silence

Hymn
Long ago the prophets knew

Response

Creed

Confession

Thanksgiving
Praise and thanks to you, Lord our God, for you give us sight and insight, eyes to see you and hearts to love you. We thank you for the beauty of the world and the glory of creation. We praise you for the many colours of nature and for the brightness of the sun. We thank you for all who have looked deeply and been aware of you and your working: we thank you for the prophets and all people of vision.
Amen.

Intercessions
Good and gracious God, open our eyes to your presence and our hearts to your love. Bless all who seek to know you and proclaim you. We remember all who study the scriptures and all who seek to be still before you. Lord, guide all who would lead us to a deep awareness of you. We ask your blessing upon all ministers and preachers and all who teach religious studies.
Lord, open our eyes to your presence
and our hearts to your love.

Lord, direct all who seek to influence our lives and our thoughts through their own vision.
Bless all who are doing research and all who are seeking to conserve what is good.

We remember before you all politicians, scientists, musicians, artists and craftspeople, and all who through their vision are enriching our lives.
Lord, open our eyes to your presence
and our hearts to your love.

Strengthen and bless all who are striving to enhance and uphold family life. Help us to see where we can increase our love and care. We remember before you all who feel neglected or lonely. May we prove to be good neighbours where we can.
Lord, open our eyes to your presence
and our hearts to your love.

We give thanks for all who have used their insight for healing and medical research. We ask your blessing upon all doctors, nurses and all involved in healing and wholeness. We bring before you friends and loved ones who are ill or struggling at this time.
Lord, open our eyes to your presence
and our hearts to your love.

Lord, extend our vision that we may know your presence and see our life as in your hands. Bless all our loved ones who are departed from us and grant that they may enjoy the vision of your glory.
Merciful Father,
accept these prayers for the sake of your Son, our Saviour Jesus Christ. Amen.

Collect

God be in my head, and in my understanding.
God be in my eyes, and in my looking.
God be in my mouth, and in my speaking.
God be in my heart, and in my thinking.
God be at my end, and at my departing.
Amen.

Sarum Book of Hours 1514

The Lord's Prayer

Silence

Hymn

God has spoken – by the prophets

Blessing

The Lord grant you a vision of his presence,
an awareness of his love,
a sensitivity to his guiding,
and the blessing of God Almighty,
the Father, the Son and the Holy Spirit
be upon you and your loved ones this day and for always.
Amen.

Advent 2
Isaiah and visionaries

Advent is a time when we rejoice in the coming of Christ into our lives, that he came at Christmas, and that he comes again to be our Lord and King. Advent celebrates that our God comes to us again and again.

Begin in the dark. If the room is not dark, close your eyes.

Welcome the light

Your word is a lamp to my feet and a light to my path.
Psalm 119:105

Lord, open our eyes to your presence.
Come, Lord of light.

Lord, open our ears to your call.
Come, Lord of light.

Lord, open our hearts to your love.
Come, Lord of light.

Lord, open our lives to your guiding.
Come, Lord of light.

Candle-lighting

On the second Sunday in Advent we light two candles, one for all of God's faithful people and one for men and women of vision. When our lives are darkened it is necessary to celebrate the presence that comes to us and the vision that is given to us.

The Lord comes to us.
He abides with us.

Light two Advent candles.

Jesus Christ is the Light of the World:
eternal light, shine in our hearts.

Blessed are you, Lord God, for you open the eyes of blind. You gave vision and insight to the prophets. We thank you for Amos and Hosea, for Isaiah, Jeremiah and Ezekiel and all the prophets, and for all people who have extended our awareness through their vision. You are their God and our God, their Father and our Father. Help us to know that as you came to them you come to us.
Blessed be God for ever.

Reading
Isaiah 6:1–8

Hymn
Be thou my vision *(first verse)*

Special intention – in the light of God

Holy God, holy and Strong One,
guide us to do what you would have us do;
inspire us to be the people you would have us be.
Lord, deliver us from lack of vision,
keep us from dullness of sight.
Help us to be true to you and ourselves
that we may live with integrity.
You give, O Lord, purpose to our days
and a meaning to our lives.
May we live to your glory
and for the good of this world.
Amen.

Closing prayer

Open my eyes, Lord, that I may see
your presence is ever with me.
Open my ears, Lord, to hear your voice
and in your will may I rejoice.
Open my heart, Lord, to your great heart
and from your love may I never depart.

Extinguish candles.

Advent 3
People immersed in God

Affirmation of God's presence

Affirmation

Advent is a time when we rejoice in the coming of Christ into our lives, that he came at Christmas, and that he comes again to be our Lord and King. Advent celebrates that our God comes to us again and again. Today is the Third Sunday in Advent, a day when we remember John the Baptist and all who turn towards God to serve him.

Invitation to worship

With John the Baptist and all God's faithful we immerse ourselves in the love, light and leading of God, Father, Son and Holy Spirit. **Amen.**

The Lord is here.
His Spirit is with us.

Hymn

Hark! a thrilling voice is sounding

Silence

Candle-lighting

On the Third Sunday in Advent we light three candles, one for all of God's faithful people, one for men and women of vision, and one for John the Baptist and all who immerse themselves in the love and presence of God.

When our lives are darkened it is necessary to celebrate the presence that comes to us and the light that is given to us.
The Lord comes to us.
He abides with us.

The lighting of the three Advent candles.

Jesus Christ is the Light of the World:
eternal light shine in our hearts.

Father you created us by your love and for your love.
May we abide in you and you in us.

Jesus you redeemed us by your love and for your love.
May we abide in you and you in us.

Spirit of God you guide us by your love and for your love.
May we abide in you and you in us.

Holy and Blessed Three your love enfolds and surrounds us.
May we abide in you and you in us.

Blessed are you, Lord our God, for you sent your messenger John the Baptist to prepare the way and make ready for your coming, that we may be prepared and ready to receive and welcome you into our lives and homes. As you come to us in love may we abide in your love and in your presence this day and for ever. Blessed be God, Father, Son and Holy Spirit.
Blessed be God for ever.

Silence

Ministry of the Word

Reading
Isaiah 40:1–11

Hymn
On Jordan's bank the Baptist's cry

The Gospel
Matthew 3:1–12

Sermon

Silence

Hymn
The advent of our King

Response

Creed

Confession

Thanksgiving
O God, we give you thanks and praise for all who have prepared the way for us to know you and to love you. We thank you for John the Baptist, that he prepared the people for the coming of Jesus. We remember in thanksgiving those who have taught us the faith by word and by example and all who have led us to you by art, music and writings. We give thanks for our baptism and the knowledge that we dwell in you and you in us. To you, O Lord our God, be praise and glory now and for ever.

Intercessions
Holy and Mighty God, as we give thanks for John the Baptist, we ask your blessing upon all who prepare the way for others to know you and to love you. Guide with your wisdom all who prepare people for baptism or confirmation. We remember all who lead worship or study groups and all who speak of your presence and your power.
Lord, may we witness
that we dwell in you and you in us.

Holy and Mighty God we give thanks for all who prepare young people to live their lives fully. We ask your blessing upon all who are involved in education, and all who influence our minds through the press, the media and their words and their actions. Guide with your wisdom all that are called to govern and to make decisions about the future of our world. Lord may we all be prepared to live simply that others might simply live. May we all work for justice, righteous dealing and for freedom.
Lord, may we witness
that we dwell in you and you in us.

Holy and Mighty God we ask your blessing upon our homes and our loved ones. We remember all who are preparing for the Christmas season and pray that they may make in their lives a place for you. We remember all who will feel lonely or neglected at this season.
Lord, may we witness
that we dwell in you and you in us.

Holy and Mighty God we give thanks for the grace of forgiveness and the opportunity to turn to you and your love. We ask your blessing upon all who are consumed with guilt or who cannot allow forgiveness for themselves or others. We remember all who are in prison and those who are suffering for their faith and their witness to you.
Lord, may we witness
that we dwell in you and you in us.

Holy and Mighty God we remember before you all who are terminally ill and are being prepared for death. May they find in you courage and hope through the promise of life eternal.
Merciful Father,
accept these prayers for the sake of your Son, Jesus Christ our Lord.
Amen.

Collect

O Lord Jesus Christ,
who at your first coming sent your messenger
to prepare your way before you:
grant that the ministers and stewards of your mysteries
may likewise so prepare and make ready your way
by turning the hearts of the disobedient
to the wisdom of the just,
that at your second coming to judge the world
we may be found an acceptable people in your sight;
for you are alive and reign with the Father
in the unity of the Holy Spirit,
one God, now and for ever.
Amen.

Common Worship Collect for Advent 3

The Lord's Prayer

Silence

Hymn
We are marching in the light of God

Blessing

The love of the Father strengthen you,
the love of Jesus surround you,
the love of the Spirit guide you,
and the blessing of God Almighty,
the Father, the Son and the Holy Spirit
be upon you and your loved ones this day and for always.
Amen.

Advent 3
John the Baptist

Advent is a time when we rejoice in the coming of Christ into our lives, that he came at Christmas, and that he comes again to be our Lord and King. Advent celebrates that our God comes to us again and again.

Begin in the dark. If the room is not dark, close your eyes.

Welcome the light

It is you who light my lamp; the Lord my God lights up my darkness.

Psalm 18:28

Rejoice, for the Lord is at hand.
Our God comes to us to give us his joy and peace.
To give us hope in our world,
hope in our hearts,
hope in our homes,
hope in our lives.
God, we rejoice at your coming
and pray that your kingdom comes in us today.

Candle-lighting

On the third Sunday in Advent we light three candles, one for all of God's faithful people, one for men and women of vision, and one for John the Baptist and all who immerse themselves in the love and presence of God.

When our lives are darkened it is necessary to celebrate the presence that comes to us and the light that is given to us.

The Lord comes to us.
He abides with us.

Light three Advent candles.

Jesus Christ is the Light of the World:
Eternal Light, shine in our hearts.

Blessed are you, Lord our God, for you sent your messenger John the Baptist to prepare the way and make ready for your coming; grant that we may be prepared and ready to receive and welcome you into our lives and homes. As you come to us in love may we abide in your love and in your presence this day and for ever. Blessed be God, Father, Son and Holy Spirit.
Blessed be God for ever.

Reading
Matthew 3:1–6

Hymn
Hark! a thrilling voice is sounding

Special intention – in the light of God

Loving God, as we give you thanks for John the Baptist,
may all peoples know they are immersed in your presence.
Bless all preachers of the word
that they may reveal that your kingdom is at hand.
Give us, O Lord, the courage to seek your will
and to strive to forward your kingdom on earth.
As your faithful people prepare for Christmas,
may they welcome you into their hearts and homes.

Closing prayer

Father, you created us by your love and for your love.
May we abide in you and you in us.

Jesus, you redeemed us by your love and for your love.
May we abide in you and you in us.

Spirit of God, you guide us by your love and for your love.
May we abide in you and you in us.

Holy and Blessed Three, your love enfolds and surrounds us.
May we abide in you and you in us.

Extinguish candles.

Advent 4
People in love with God

Affirmation of God's presence

Affirmation
Advent is a time when we rejoice in the coming of Christ into our lives, that he came at Christmas, and that he comes again to be our Lord and King. Advent celebrates that our God comes to us again and again. Today is the Fourth Sunday in Advent when we remember the Blessed Virgin Mary and give thanks for all who love God and seek to do his will.

Invitation to worship
With the Blessed Virgin Mary we rejoice in the God who comes to us. We are in power and presence of God, Father, Son and Holy Spirit.
Amen.

The Lord is here.
His Spirit is with us.

Hymn
Love divine, all loves excelling

Silence

Candle-lighting

On the Fourth Sunday in Advent we light four candles, one for all of God's faithful people, one for men and women of vision, and one for John the Baptist and all who immerse themselves in the love and presence of God. The fourth candle is for the Blessed Virgin Mary and all who give themselves to God in love.

When our lives are darkened it is necessary to celebrate the presence that comes to us and the light that is given to us.
The Lord comes to us.
He abides with us.

The lighting of the four Advent candles.

Jesus Christ is the Light of the World:
eternal light shine in our hearts.

In Christ Jesus the darkness is defeated:
the light has come into the world. *Light candle one.*
Emmanuel, God is with us.

In Christ Jesus a new day has dawned:
the light has come into the world. *Light candle two.*
Emmanuel, God is with us.

In Christ Jesus is our hope and joy:
the light has come into the world. *Light candle three.*
Emmanuel, God is with us.

In Christ Jesus life is eternal:
the light has come into the world. *Light candle four.*
Emmanuel, God is with us.

Blessed are you Lord our God, for in the fullness of time you shared in our humanity being born of the Blessed Virgin Mary. You came down to lift us up: you became human that we might share in the divine. As we rejoice in Mary doing your will and so welcoming you into her life may we abide in you and know that you abide in us.
Blessed are you Father, Son and Holy Spirit.
Blessed be God for ever.

Silence

Ministry of the Word

Reading
Isaiah 7:10 –15

Hymn
Tell out, my soul

The Gospel
Luke 1:26–38

Sermon

Silence

Hymn
O come, O come, Emmanuel

Response

Creed

Confession

Thanksgiving
Lord God we give you thanks and praise for the angel Gabriel and the message he brought to Mary. We thank you for her acceptance, her obedience and her joy. We rejoice that through Mary our Saviour came to dwell among us.

May we learn the obedience of Mary, serving you with joy and accepting Jesus into our lives. We rejoice that you are her God and our God: you are her Father and our Father. Help us to know that as you came to Mary you come to us and through us your will can be done.

Intercessions

O God, as we celebrate your coming among us, we seek to give our love to you. In our daily living let us seek to do your will and help to bring in your kingdom.

Through all who seek to obey to you,
through all who quietly witness to your presence,
through our faithfulness in prayer,
through our working for your glory,
through all reaching out in mission,
in our love and obedience,
your kingdom come.

Through all who desire righteousness and freedom,
through all who strive for peace,
through all that are caring for the poor,
through those who seek to improve your world,
in our love and obedience,
your kingdom come.

Through all our relationships,
through our love in our homes,
through our community and our society,
through our daily work and our talents,
in our love and obedience,
your kingdom come.

Through those who provide places of healing and shelter,
through the caring professions,
through all who look after the ill and lonely,
through all who show compassion and care,
in our love and obedience,
your kingdom come.

We remember especially today the love and obedience of Mary and ask your prayers for all faithful people. We remember loved ones and friends who are now departed from us; may they rejoice in your eternal kingdom.
Merciful Father,
accept these prayers for the sake of your Son, Jesus Christ our Lord.
Amen.

Collect

God our redeemer,
who prepared the Blessed Virgin Mary
to be the mother of your Son:
grant that, as she looked for his coming as our Saviour,
so we may be ready to greet him
when he comes again as our judge;
who is alive and reigns with you,
in the unity of the Holy Spirit,
one God, now and for ever.
Amen.

Common Worship Collect for Advent 4

The Lord's Prayer

Silence

Hymn

It is a thing most wonderful

Blessing

God give you grace to follow the example of Mary
and to welcome the Christ into your lives and homes.
The Holy Spirit overshadow you and protect you,
and the blessing of God Almighty,
the Father, the Son and the Holy Spirit
be upon you and your loved ones this day and for always.
Amen.

Advent 4
The Blessed Virgin Mary

Advent is a time when we rejoice in the coming of Christ into our lives, that he came at Christmas, and that he comes again to be our Lord and King. Advent celebrates that our God comes to us again and again.

Begin in the dark. If the room is not dark, close your eyes.

Welcome the light

In him was life, and the life was the light of all people. The light shines in the darkness, and the darkness did not overcome it.

John 1:4, 5

In Christ Jesus the darkness is defeated:
his light has come into the world.
Emmanuel, God is with us.

In Christ Jesus a new day has dawned:
his light has come into the world.
Emmanuel, God is with us.

In Christ Jesus is our hope and joy:
his light has come into the world.
Emmanuel, God is with us.

In Christ Jesus life is eternal:
his light has come into the world.
Emmanuel, God is with us.

Candle-lighting

On the fourth Sunday in Advent we light four candles, one for all of God's faithful people, one for men and women of vision, and one for John the Baptist and all who immerse themselves in the love and presence of God. The fourth candle is for the Blessed Virgin Mary and all who give themselves to God in love.

When our lives are darkened it is necessary to celebrate the presence that comes to us and the light that is given to us.

The Lord comes to us.
He abides with us.

Light four Advent candles.

Jesus Christ is the Light of the World;
eternal light, shine in our hearts.

Blessed are you, Lord our God, for in the fullness of time you shared in our humanity, being born of the Blessed Virgin Mary. You came down to lift us up; you became human that we might share in the divine. As we rejoice in Mary doing your will and so welcoming you into her life may we abide in you and know that you abide in us.
Blessed are you Father, Son and Holy Spirit.
Blessed be God for ever.

Reading
Isaiah 7:10–14

Hymn
Hark the glad sound

Special intention – in the light of God

We bring before you, O Lord,
all whose lives are darkened.
We remember the poor and the homeless,
all who are ill and suffering,
those who are approaching death,
and all who have lost loved ones.

Lord be known to them, come as the light,
let your peace fill them and your love enfold them.
We ask this for you love and mercy's sake.
Amen.

Closing prayer

O Light that lightens our way,
let us not fear the darkness of this day.
To open to you is to welcome the Light.
To walk in your light is to know eternal life.
Come, Lord Jesus, be known to all who walk in darkness.
Come, Lord Jesus, you are our light and our salvation.
Come, Lord of life.

Extinguish candles.

17 December

O Sapientia
The wisdom of God

Begin in the dark. If the room is not dark, close your eyes.

Welcome the light

O Wisdom coming out from the Most High, filling all creation and reigning to the ends of the earth: come and teach us the way of truth.
Amen.
Come, Lord Jesus.

Candle-lighting

He is the source of your life in Christ Jesus, who became for us wisdom from God, and righteousness and sanctification and redemption.
1 Corinthians 1:30

Come, Lord, with your grace and goodness:
come to our hearts and change us.
Come, wisdom of God.
Come, Christ our Lord.

Come, Lord, with your peace and power:
come to our lives and strengthen us.
Come, wisdom of God.
Come, Christ our Lord.

Come, Lord, with your light and love:
come to our darkness and enlighten us.
Come, wisdom of God.
Come, Christ our Lord.

Jesus Christ, the wisdom of God, is the Light of the World.
A light that no darkness can quench.

Light the candle.

Blessed are you, Lord our God, for in your wisdom you have created us and by your wisdom you have redeemed us. Blessed are you Father, Son and Holy Spirit.
Blessed be God for ever.

Reading
Proverbs 2:1–15

Hymn
O come, O come, Emmanuel *(second verse and refrain)*

Special intention – in the light of God

O wisdom, issuing out of the mouth of God;
maranatha.
Come, Lord Jesus.

O wisdom, the very breath and power of God;
maranatha.
Come, Lord Jesus.

O wisdom, the image and goodness of God;
maranatha.
Come, Lord Jesus.

O wisdom, passing into holy souls;
maranatha.
Come, Lord Jesus.

O wisdom, working in the prophets;
maranatha.
Come, Lord Jesus.

O wisdom, triumphing over evil;
maranatha.
Come, Lord Jesus.

O wisdom, dancing in creation;
maranatha.
Come, Lord Jesus.

Closing prayer

God, give us grace to accept with serenity
the things that cannot be changed,
the courage to change the things that should be changed,
and the wisdom to know the difference.
Reinhold Niebuhr 1892–1971

O Wisdom, coming out from the Most High,
filling all creation and reigning to the ends of the earth:
come and teach us the way of truth.
Amen.
Come, Lord Jesus.

May the Lord when he comes find us watching and waiting.

Extinguish candle.

18 December

O Adonai

The Lord of lords

Begin in the dark. If the room is not dark, close your eyes.

Welcome the light

O Lord of lords and leader of the house of Israel, you appeared to Moses in the fire of the burning bush and gave your law on Sinai; come and save us with your mighty arm and redeem us.
Amen.
Come, Lord Jesus.

Lord of the burning bush,
scatter our darkness and make yourself known to us;
maranatha.
Come, Lord Jesus.

Lord of the desert,
lead us to the waters of life;
maranatha.
Come, Lord Jesus.

Lord of the Rock,
shelter us and protect us;
maranatha.
Come, Lord Jesus.

Lord of the living water,
refresh and restore us;
maranatha.
Come, Lord Jesus.

Lord of the manna,
strengthen and sustain us;
maranatha.
Come, Lord Jesus.

Lord of Mount Sinai,
Direct and guide us;
maranatha.
Come, Lord Jesus.

Lord, our Friend and Saviour,
redeem us and bring us to the Promised Land;
maranatha.
Come, Lord Jesus.

Candle-lighting

Jesus Christ our Lord is the Light of the World.
A light no darkness can put out.

Light the candle.

Blessed are you, Lord God Almighty, for you have revealed your presence to us through prophets, saints and holy people. As you made yourself known to Moses may we know that you are with us and abide with us in our journeying. Blessed are you, Father, Son and Holy Spirit.
Blessed be God for ever.

Reading
Exodus 3:1–6

Hymn
O come, O come, Emmanuel *(third verse and refrain)*

Special intention – in the light of God

Lord, teach us and all peoples to live by your law of love.
Guide us in our journeying through life;
strengthen and sustain all who are struggling;
shield and shelter us until we enter the fullness of your kingdom.
We ask this in the love of our Lord, Jesus Christ.
Amen.

Closing prayer

The leading of the Lord go before us.
The light of the Lord be about us.
The love of the Lord enfold us.
Now and for evermore.
O Lord of lords and leader of the house of Israel,
you appeared to Moses in the fire of the burning bush
and gave your law on Sinai;
come and save us with your mighty arm and redeem us.
Amen.
Come, Lord Jesus.

May the Lord when he comes find us watching and waiting.

Extinguish candle.

19 December

O Radix Jesse
The Root of Jesse

Begin in the dark. If the room is not dark, close your eyes.

Welcome the light

O Root of Jesse, standing as a sign among the nations: kings will keep silence before you for whom the nations long: come and save us and delay no longer.
Amen.
Come Lord, Jesus.

Blessed be the Lord the God of Israel,
who has come to his people and set them free.
Blessed be the Lord the God of Israel.

He has raised up for us a mighty Saviour,
born of the house of his servant David.
Blessed be the Lord the God of Israel.

Glory be to the Father, the Son, and the Holy Spirit.
Blessed be the Lord the God of Israel.
Benedictus from Luke 1:68–69

Candle-lighting

Jesus Christ is the Light of the World.
A light that no darkness can extinguish.

Light the candle.

Blessed are you Lord God, King of Glory,
revealed in the face of our Lord Jesus Christ;
revealed in him who is born of the house of David:
revealed in the Light that scatters our darkness;
revealed in him that is the hope of all the world.
Blessed are you, Lord our God, now and for ever.

Reading
Isaiah 11:1–4a, 6–10

Hymn
O come, O come, Emmanuel *(fourth verse and refrain)*

Special intention – in the light of God

Jesus, Word made flesh;
maranatha.
Come, Lord, dwell among us.

Jesus, born of the house of David;
maranatha.
Come, Lord, dwell among us.

Jesus, born of the blessed Virgin Mary;
maranatha.
Come, Lord, dwell among us.

Jesus, sharing in our humanity;
maranatha.
Come, Lord, dwell among us.

Closing prayer

Jesus, born of Mary, bless all parents in their care for their children.
Jesus, born in a stable, be a strength to all who are homeless.
Jesus, taken into Egypt, be known among the refugees and migrants.
Jesus, sharing in our humanity,
bring us to know the mystery of your divinity.

Jesus, King of Glory,
help us to know you are with us now and always.
O root of Jesse, standing as a sign among the nations:
kings will keep silence before you for whom the nations long.
Come and save us and delay no longer.
Amen.
Come Lord, Jesus.

May the Lord when he comes find us watching and waiting.

Extinguish candle.

20 December

O Clavis David
The Key of David

Begin in the dark. If the room is not dark, close your eyes.

Welcome the light

O Key of David and sceptre of the House of Israel; you open and none can shut; you shut and none can open. Come, free the captives from prison, and break down the walls of death.
Amen.
Come, Lord Jesus.

O Key of David,
you open to us your love.
Come, Lord,
be known among us.

O Key of David,
you come to set the prisoner free.
Come, Lord,
be known among us.

O Key of David,
you open to us the kingdom of heaven.
Come, Lord,
be known among us.

O Key of David,
you open to us eternal life.
Come, Lord,
be known among us.

Candle-lighting

Jesus Christ is the Light of the World.
A light that no darkness can extinguish.

Light the candle.

Blessed are you, Lord our God, for in your grace and goodness you sent your Son into the world and he has opened for us the kingdom of heaven. We give you thanks for every opportunity you set before us to know and love you. Open our eyes to your presence and our hearts to your love. Blessed are you Father, Son and Holy Spirit.
Blessed be God for ever.

Reading

Revelation 3:7; 5:2–5

Hymn

O come, O come, Emmanuel *(fifth verse and refrain)*

Special intention – in the light of God

Christ, Key of David, we bring before you
all who are locked in on themselves:
we bring all prisoners,
all who are bound by addiction,
all who are held by vice,
all who are captives to habit,
all who are restricted by their environment,
all who suffer from tyranny,
all who feel trapped by life.
Jesus, we come to you, our Redeemer,
for in your love you seek to release those who are bound.

Closing prayer

Loving Lord,
open our eyes to your presence,
open our ears to your call,
open our hearts to your love.
O Key of David and sceptre of the House of Israel;
you open and none can shut; you shut and none can open:
come, free the captives from prison,
and break down the walls of death.
Amen.
Come, Lord Jesus.

May the Lord when he comes find us watching and waiting.

Extinguish candle.

21 December

O Oriens
Christ the Morning Star

Begin in the dark. If the room is not dark, close your eyes.

Welcome the light

O morning star, splendour of the light eternal and bright sun of righteousness: come with your light to all who dwell in darkness and in the shadow of death.
Amen.
Come, Lord Jesus.

Arise and shine; for your light has come,
the glory of the Lord has risen upon you.
Arise and shine for your light has come.

For darkness shall cover the earth,
and thick darkness the peoples.
Arise and shine for your light has come.

But the Lord will arise upon you,
and his glory will appear over you.
Arise and shine for your light has come.

Nations shall come to your light
and kings to the brightness of your dawn.
Arise and shine for your light has come.

Glory be to the Father, and to the Son, and to the Holy Spirit.
Arise and shine for your light has come.

Isaiah 60:1–3

Christ is the Morning Star,
who, when the night of this world is past,
brings to his saints the promise of the light
of life and opens everlasting day.
Bede 671–735

Candle-lighting

Blessed are you, Lord our God,
Creator of light out of darkness.
In this season of Advent, when the sun's light is swallowed up,
by the increasing darkness of night,
you offer us the splendour of your glory,
revealed in Christ our Morning Star.
Through him you call us to be children of the day
and not of the night, and to walk in the presence of he who is the Light of the World, even Christ our Lord.
Blessed are you Father, Son and Holy Spirit.
Blessed be God for ever.

Light the candle.

Readings

Psalm 107:10–14; Luke 1:78, 79; Revelation 22:16

Hymn

O come, O come, Emmanuel *(sixth verse and refrain)*

Special intention – in the light of God

Christ as a light illumine and guide me,
Christ as shield overshadow me,
Christ be under me, Christ be over me,
Christ beside me, on my left and my right.
This day be within and without me;
lowly and meek, yet all-powerful.

Be to the heart of each one to whom I speak;
in the mouth of each who speaks unto me;
lowly and meek, yet all powerful.
Christ as a light, Christ as shield,
Christ beside me on my left and my right.
Attributed to St Patrick

Closing prayer

O Christ, our Morning Star,
Splendour of Light Eternal,
shining with the glory of the rainbow,
come and waken us,
from the greyness of our apathy
and renew us with your gift of hope.
Bede 671–735

O Morning Star,
splendour of the light eternal and bright sun of righteousness:
come with your light to all who dwell in darkness
and in the shadow of death.
Amen.
Come, Lord Jesus.

May the Lord when he comes find us watching and waiting.

Extinguish candle.

22 December

O Rex Gentium

King of the nations

Begin in the dark. If the room is not dark, close your eyes.

Welcome the light

O King of the nations, you alone can fulfil their desires: Cornerstone; binding all together, come and save the creature you have fashioned from the earth.
Amen.
Come, Lord Jesus.

Great and amazing are your deeds, Lord God the Almighty.
We watch for you, we wait for you.

Just and true are your ways, O King of the nations!
We watch for you, we wait for you.

Lord, who will not fear and glorify your name?
For you alone are holy.
We watch for you, we wait for you.

All nations shall come and worship before you,
for your judgements have been revealed.
We watch for you, we wait for you.

Revelation 15:3b, 4

Candle-lighting

Jesus Christ is the Light of the World.
A light that no darkness can extinguish.

Light the candle.

Blessed are you, Lord our God, for you have created all things.
you created us out of love and for your love.
you sent your Son to be our Saviour.
He lived among us and faced death that we might know eternal life.
Now he is the King of kings and Lord of lords
and in seeking to do his will we are one with him in his kingdom.
We look for the time when the kingdoms of the world
will become the kingdom of Christ our Lord.
Blessed are you Father, Son and Holy Spirit.
Blessed be God for ever.

Reading
Jeremiah 30:7–11a; Acts 4:10–12

Hymn
O come, O come, Emmanuel *(seventh verse and refrain)*

Special intention – in the light of God

Come to your world, O King of the nations.
We look for you: we long for you.

Christ our King, let your word be a light to our feet, a lantern to our path.
We look for you: we long for you.

Christ our King, come and rule in our hearts.
We look for you: we long for you.

Christ our King, come, be known to all people in all places.
We look for you: we long for you.

Come, that the kingdoms of the world may become the kingdom of Christ.
We look for you: we long for you.

Closing prayer

Lord, your kingdom come as in heaven.
Come in my heart, Lord,
come in my actions,
come in my mind,
come in my whole life,
come, High King of heaven.
For in your coming heaven and earth become one.
Lord, your kingdom come as in heaven.
O King of the nations, you alone can fulfil their desires:
Cornerstone; binding all together,
come and save the creature you have fashioned from the earth.
Amen.
Come, Lord Jesus.

May the Lord when he comes find us watching and waiting.

Extinguish candle.

23 December

O Emmanuel
God with us

Begin in the dark. If the room is not dark, close your eyes.

Welcome the light

O Emmanuel, our King and our Lawgiver, hope of the nations and their Saviour: come and save us, O Lord our God.
Amen.
Come, Lord Jesus.

O Emmanuel, God with us,
open our eyes to your presence.
Come, Lord Jesus.

Make our homes your home.
Come, Lord Jesus.

Make room in our lives for you.
Come, Lord Jesus.

O Emmanuel, God ever present,
reveal your self to us.
Come, Lord Jesus.

Candle-lighting

Jesus Christ is the Light of the World.
A light that no darkness can quench.

Light the candle.

Reading
Matthew 1:18–23

Hymn

O come, O come, Emmanuel *(first verse and refrain)*

Special intention – in the light of God

Our Lord says, 'Surely I am coming quickly.' Even so come, Lord Jesus.
Come, dwell among us.

O Wisdom, filling all of creation, come and make us friends of God.
Come, dwell among us.

O Lord of lords, who appeared to Moses in the burning bush, come and make yourself known to us.
Come, dwell among us.

O Root of Jesse, taking upon you our humanity that we may share in your divinity,
come, dwell among us.

Key of David, when you open no one can close; come bring us to the glorious liberty of the children of God.
Come, dwell among us.

O Morning Star, Splendour of eternal light,
come give light to all who walk in darkness and in the shadow of death.
Come, dwell among us.

O King of the nations, ruler we long for, come in love and peace to save your people.
Come, dwell among us.

O Emmanuel, God ever present, make yourself known to us.
Come, dwell among us.

Closing prayer

O Emmanuel, our King and our Lawgiver,
hope of the nations and their Saviour:
come and save us, O Lord our God.
Amen.
Come, Lord Jesus.

May the Lord when he comes find us watching and waiting.

Extinguish candle.

Christmas

Carol service

Material needed: Advent wreath, or five candles plus one more candle; crib figures including an angel, wise men optional. Candles with drip shields for everyone optional.

Carol

Once in royal David's city

This holy night (day), we give thanks for the coming of the Lord of Glory. Jesus not only comes to Bethlehem, he comes to us, today. He comes to our world, our homes, and our loved ones. Let us make room for him and rejoice at his coming. Come and share in the love of Mary and Joseph: join in the song of the angels and share in the wonder of the shepherds. Above all let us give ourselves to him, for he gives himself to us.

The hope of glory

Reading

Isaiah 9:2, 6, 7

Prayer

Father, on this holy night (day) our Saviour came as light into our darkness and revealed his love for the whole world. Open our eyes to his presence and our hearts to his love that we may know him as the Prince of Peace and Lord of Light.

The lighting of the four Advent candles

Have four people, with lighted tapers, come from different corners of the church. (This can be more effective if the lights are left off until the Advent candles are lit, or off all the time if it is a service by candlelight.)

Let the first person begin by saying, 'Emmanuel' and asking the congregation to say, **'The Lord is with us. Amen'** every time it is said and to say it loudly. In turn let the people with tapers come down the church and light a single candle. After each one lights a candle they say 'Emmanuel' and the congregation respond.

As the four people light the candles, each has a sentence to say:

The Christ is come into the world.
Emmanuel,
the Lord is with us. Amen.

Jesus is born among us.
Emmanuel,
the Lord is with us. Amen.

Our God has taken upon him our flesh.
Emmanuel,
the Lord is with us. Amen.

This is the light that defeats the darkness.
Emmanuel,
the Lord is with us. Amen.

Prayer

Blessed are you Lord our God for in your deep love for us you have shared in our humanity that we might share in your glory. Help us to make room in our lives to be aware of you and of your coming to us through Jesus Christ the Word made flesh. **Amen.**

Carol

Of the Father's love begotten

Glory in the darkness

Reading

John 1:1–5

The lighting of the Christ candle

This night (day) the Saviour promised long is come.
Emmanuel,
the Lord is with us. Amen.

The Saviour comes among us and is here.
Emmanuel,
the Lord is with us. Amen.

His light shines in darkness that is about us.

Light the candle.

Emmanuel,
the Lord is with us. Amen.

Prayer
Father on this holy night (day) made resplendent with the glory of the true Light, grant that we who have known the mystery of that Light on earth, may enter into the fullness of his joys in heaven. **Amen.**

Ancient Western Rite, adapted

If the service is to be by candlelight then let everyone have their candles lit from the Christ candle or from a person who has passed on this light.

Carol
Silent night

The promise of glory

Reading
Luke 1:26–38

Prayer
Father on this holy night (day) your promise to Mary is fulfilled. Jesus Christ our Saviour comes down and takes upon him our flesh. As he shares in our humanity may we share in his divinity through him who is Christ the Lord.

Carol
O little town of Bethlehem

During the carol Joseph and Mary are placed in the stable.

Glory in the night

Reading
Luke 2:1–7

Prayer
Father on this holy night (day) Joseph and Mary could find no room at the inn and the Christ was born in the stable. We remember before you all who are homeless, all poor people and refugees.

Lord, hear us.
Lord, mercifully hear us.

Carol
Away in a manger

Jesus is brought and placed in the stable.

Angels of glory

Reading
Luke 2:8–14

Prayer
Father on this holy night (day) the holy angels sang 'Peace on earth and good will to all'. Grant us your peace, Lord, in our hearts and in our homes: peace in all our dealings and peace in our world.
Lord, hear us.
Lord, mercifully hear us.

Carol
Hark, the herald-angels sing

The Angel is placed above the stable. If the crib set does not have an angel cut some from old Christmas cards and at this point have them placed above the crib. Though there are many beautiful Christmas angels that could be bought to add to your crib.

Glory come to earth

Reading

Luke 2:15–20

Prayer

Father on this holy night (day) the shepherds heard the songs of angels. They travelled to Bethlehem to see Jesus and they gave to you praise and glory for all they had seen and heard. Make us aware of the presence of our Lord that we also may give you praise and glory. We remember all whose lives are shrouded with darkness and who need the light of Christ.
Lord, hear us.
Lord, mercifully hear us.

Carol

While shepherds watched

The shepherds and sheep are placed in the stable.

Glory for everyone

Reading

Matthew 2:1–12

Prayer

Father on this holy night (day) your love was revealed for all people in all places. We ask your blessing upon all pilgrim people and all who are seekers.
Lord, hear us.
Lord, mercifully hear us.

Carol

We three kings of Orient are
The kings can be placed on window sills around the church or at various points as they are still meant to be travelling. A lit candle is placed near the stable to represent us, because we love Jesus and we know he loves us.

We have seen his glory

Reading
John 10–14

Blessed are you, Lord our God, for you have revealed your glory and your love in the face of our Lord Jesus Christ: for us and for our salvation he has come to dwell among us. He has shared in our humanity that we might share in his divinity. Blessed are you Father, Son and Holy Spirit.

As our Saviour has taught us, so we pray:
(The Lord's Prayer)

The blessing of the crib

God our Father, we thank you for Jesus born
of the Blessed Virgin Mary and that he came to live among us.
As we rejoice in his birth,
we ask you to bless this crib
that all who see it may be reminded of your love
and your presence with us.
May it help to bring his light into the darkness of our world:
through the same Christ who abides with us
and reigns with you and the Holy Spirit, one God now and for ever.
Amen.

Carol
O come, all ye faithful

Blessing

Give glory to God who loves us with an everlasting love.
The presence of the Mighty God be with you,
the love of the Everlasting Father enfold you,
the peace of the Prince of Peace surround you,
the light of the Wonderful Counsellor guide you,
and the blessing of God Almighty, the Father, the Son and the Holy Spirit, be upon you and your homes and loved ones now and for evermore. **Amen.**

The Christmas story

Materials needed: a set of crib figures, including an angel, and two candles. Let the teller of the story sit as close to the children as possible for the readings. I usually place my script inside a large Christmas card.

Welcome the light

Welcome to you all who have come to give thanks to God for his love and for Jesus being born into the world. We will begin by being very quiet.

We are in the presence and in the love of God,
Father, Son and Holy Spirit.
The Lord is with you.
And also with you.

Lord Jesus, help us to love you like Mary and Joseph,
to worship with the angels,
to come to you with the shepherds,
to give our lives to you like the wise men.
Help us to celebrate your birthday with joy.

There was no room for you at the inn –
let us make room in our hearts for you.
You were born in a stable –
we pray for all without a home or people to love them.
Mary and Joseph gave you a home – bless our homes today.
The angels sang your praises – may we sing to you with joy.
The shepherds came to see you – may we seek to know you.
You came because you love us – help us to love you.

Christ, our Lord, come to earth,
bless our homes by your birth.
Christ born in a manger stall,
bless our loved ones one and all.
Christ a baby, yet God and King,
bless us now as to you we sing.

Carol

O little town of Bethlehem

The Christmas story

Once a very long time ago there was a little town called 'The House of Bread' – we call it Bethlehem. There in the quiet of the night the wonderful Christmas story happened.

Now in the village of Bethlehem there was an inn, a place where people could come and stay. We do not know its name but let us pretend we can hear its sign creaking as it swings in the wind. The innkeeper should have put some oil on it but he has been too busy for the inn is full of people. It would be hard to make room for any more. This is because the government has made a law that everyone must go to the place where they were born and there have their name written down in a big book. There were lots and lots of people on all of the roads. The inn was already packed full. Inside there was singing and dancing. People were meeting family and friends and telling stories. It was all very busy and noisy.

But outside it was still and quiet. Out of the back door, past the well where they got water, past the sleeping hens, the goats and the sheep there was a stable, a cattle shed. It was quiet there except for the sound of the cow and the donkey breathing. Imagine their warm breath coming out of their mouths, for it was a cold night. From the stable you can see the stars shining. One very bright star seems to be shining right on to the stable. (While we sing our carol the cow and the donkey will go to the stable.) 1st v.

Carol

Little donkey

So there in the quiet the animals rest and wait, breathing quietly in the cold night air. A bright star shines upon them.

Let us go again to the front of the inn. We stand under the sign and look down the road. The road shines in the moonlight. Two people are coming down the road very slowly. They look like shadows in the distance. As they come nearer we see they are a man and a young woman. They have come a long way and the woman is very tired. They can only move slowly for the woman is going to have a baby.

We know what no one in Bethlehem knows, the baby will be born tonight. The man is Joseph the Carpenter, who makes things with wood. The lady is Mary and soon she is to be the mother of the baby Jesus.

They look at the creaking sign and then they knock hard on the door. For a while no one comes. At last the innkeeper comes wiping his hands. He has too many people to look after. There is no room for any more. He is sorry but he cannot help. Almost as he closed the door he stopped. Mary and Joseph looked so tired, he was sorry for them. He said, 'You can sleep in the stable if you want to. You will have to share it with the animals.' Mary and Joseph were so relieved. The innkeeper showed them around the side of the inn. As they passed the well they could hear the singing and dancing of the crowds. They went past the sheep and the goats into the quiet stable. It looked as if it had been waiting for them. Mary thought this would be a better place than a crowded inn for her baby to be born. The cow and the donkey looked up as if to welcome them. The innkeeper gave them a lantern light and left them to settle down for the night. While we sing our next carol Mary and Joseph will be taken and placed in the stable. 2nd v.

Carol
Silent night

The cow and the donkey, Mary and Joseph are settled in the stable. There by the light of the lantern we watch big shadows dancing on the walls. It looks as if darkness and light are having a fight. Suddenly a baby cries – for Jesus is born. God who loves us and all the world has sent his Son into the world. Jesus is born of Mary. As his mother, Mary will look after him. With Joseph's help Jesus is washed. Then his little body is rubbed gently with salt! That is to be like a medicine to stop Jesus being poorly. Then Jesus is carefully wrapped up in bands of cloth to keep him safe and warm. He is sleepy so Joseph puts him in the manger of hay to sleep.

Look, here is the baby Jesus for the crib. See how tiny he looks in this church, but not as tiny as Jesus looked in the great big dark world. While we sing our next carol the baby Jesus will be carefully carried and put in the stable. We will also light a candle . . . It goes to stand beside the stable to show that a special light has come into the world. This light tells us of the love of God. This is the light of Jesus Christ.

[illegible] verse · 5

Carol

Away in a manger

Now away from the inn and high up on the hillsides it was dark and cold. There in the night, men were working. They were shepherds and they were looking after their sheep in the dark. They were very brave for they were guarding their sheep against wolves or robbers. They were keeping watch, looking out on the night. Some were sitting close to a fire to keep warm. It was a cold night and the stars shone like jewels in the sky. Isaac, that is the name of one of the shepherds, threw a large piece of wood onto the fire. It caused sparks to fly upwards, they rose higher and higher as if they were trying to reach the stars. Suddenly the light grew brighter, it was as if the sparks were taking on a shape, and there was something strange in the sky. The light got brighter and it was coming nearer and nearer. Isaac wondered if he was dreaming – now he was afraid. What was it? Then there was the most beautiful singing that he had ever heard. Voices from out of this world, for angels were singing a lovely song. The shepherds were very still and listened to the words, 'Glory to God in the highest and on earth peace. Glory to God in the highest and on earth peace.'

Look, here is our angel. Let us all be still and quiet while it is taken to be near the stable.

Carol

The Virgin Mary had a baby boy

The brave shepherds were afraid. But an angel said, 'Do not be afraid for I bring you good news – good tidings of great joy. This will make you happy. Today, this very night, in Bethlehem, the city of David, a Saviour is born. It is Christ the Lord. God has sent him because he loves you and all people. Go to Bethlehem and this is what you will find: a baby wrapped up in bands of cloth and lying in a manger. The angel stopped speaking and again the shepherds heard the angels' song, 'Glory to God in the highest and on earth peace.' Then it was suddenly very quiet because the angels had gone. The night was dark again and the shepherds were all alone on the hillside. They rubbed their eyes and looked at the sky and then at each other. They wondered if they had dreamt it but it was real.

'Come,' said one of them, 'let us go to Bethlehem and see this wonderful baby.' So taking their shepherd's crooks and their youngest sheepdog they set off. The older dogs were left to protect the sheep. By now Bethlehem was very quiet; everyone was sleeping, or trying to, except for Mary and Joseph who were looking after the baby.

During the singing of our next carol the shepherds will make their way to the stable to see Jesus.

Carol

While shepherds watched

The shepherds tiptoed across the rustling straw and bowed down to look at the little baby. They all stood very quiet and still just looking at Jesus. They were all giving their love to the baby. Mary his mother, Joseph who would look after Mary and the baby, and the shepherds; all of them worshipping Jesus. This is what we are called to do, to be quiet before Jesus and to give our love to him. We are to make our church like the stable at Bethlehem and worship the newborn King. It is here that Jesus comes to us, he wants to give his love to us and for us to give our love to him. Let us close our eyes, and hear again the song of the angels, 'Glory to God in the highest and on earth peace.' They say to us, 'To you is born this day in the city of David, in Bethlehem, a Saviour who is Christ the Lord.' Let us be still and quiet and say thank you to God for Jesus and to Jesus for coming to live on earth.

While we sing someone will light a candle from the Jesus candle and put it near the crib. This candle is for us because we love Jesus and we know he loves us.

Now let us sing:
O come, let us adore him,
O come, let us adore him,
O come, let us adore him,
Christ the Lord.

The blessing of the crib

Praise and thanks to you, Lord our God, for you have sent your Son, Jesus, to come into the world. We thank you for Mary and Joseph and their love for Jesus. We thank you for the angels and for the shepherds and for all who welcomed Jesus into the world. May we also give our love to him this day and always.

As Jesus our Saviour has taught us, so we pray:
(The Lord's Prayer)

God our Father, we thank you for Jesus born
of the Blessed Virgin Mary and that he came to live among us.
As we rejoice in his birth,
we ask you to bless this crib
that all who see it may be reminded of your love
and your presence with us.
May it help to bring his light into the darkness of our world:
through the same Christ who abides with us
and reigns with you and the Holy Spirit, one God now and for ever.
Amen.

Carol
O come, all ye faithful

Blessing

God go with you and be known in your homes;
let Christ our Lord be known to live among you;
the Holy Spirit of God go with you and guide you
and the blessing of God Almighty,
the Father, the Son and the Holy Spirit be upon you
and your loved ones this day and for always.
Amen.

Christmas Eve

Begin in the dark. If the room is not dark, close your eyes.

Welcome the light

What has come into being in him was life, and the life was the light of all people. The light shines in the darkness and the darkness has not overcome it.

John 1:4, 5

The Eternal Word, born of the Father before time began, today emptied himself for our sake and became one of us.

Evening Prayer, Christmas Eve

This holy night, the darkness is scattered,
for the King of Glory comes to dwell among us.
This holy night Christ comes to earth;
in him heaven and earth are one.
This holy night we join the angels in praise
singing, 'Glory to God on high and on earth peace.'
This holy night let us join with the shepherds
and come and kneel before the Christ child.

Candle-lighting

Jesus Christ is the Light of the World.
The light that no darkness can quench.

The Light of Christ.
Thanks be to God.

Light the candle.

Blessed is Jesus, the Lord our Saviour:
blessed is he who shared our humanity,
that we might partake of his divinity.
Blessed is he who became a mortal that we might know eternal life.
Blessed is he who became poor to enrich us all.
Blessed is he who fulfilled the dreams and visions of the prophets.
Blessed is he who is the Babe of Bethlehem yet King of kings
and Lord of lords.
Blessed is Jesus, the Lord our Saviour.

O God, who made this most hallowed night
resplendent with the glory of the true Light,
grant that we who have known the mystery of that Light on earth,
may enter into the fullness of his joys in heaven.

Ancient Western Rite

Reading
Luke 2:8–20

Hymn
In the bleak midwinter *(final verse)*

Special intention – in the light of God

Lord Jesus, babe of Bethlehem,
we ask your blessing upon all newborn children.
Lord Jesus, born in a stable,
give hope and courage to all who are homeless and poor.
Lord Jesus, soon to become a refugee because of Herod,
give strength to all who are persecuted and who suffer from violence.
Lord Jesus, King of Glory, with the angels and shepherds,
we adore you and rejoice in your coming among us.
Lord Jesus, as you came out of love for us,
we seek to give our love and our lives to you.

Closing prayer

This holy night you, Lord, come down and dwell among us.
Heaven and earth are one in you.
God and our humanity are united.
The heavenly glory is seen in human flesh.
Darkness is conquered by the Light of the World.
You, Lord, are one with us.
May we go on our way rejoicing.

Extinguish candle.

Christmas Day

Begin in the dark. If the room is not dark, close your eyes.

Welcome the light

The Word became flesh and lived among us, and we have seen his glory, the glory as of a father's only son, full of grace and truth.

John 1:14

The following affirmation can be used while four Advent candles are lit or simply as a rejoicing before the lighting of the Christ Candle.

The Christ is come into the world. Emmanuel,
the Lord is with us. Amen.

Jesus is born among us. Emmanuel,
the Lord is with us. Amen.

Our God has taken upon him our flesh. Emmanuel,
the Lord is with us. Amen.

This is the light that defeats the darkness. Emmanuel,
the Lord is with us. Amen.

Candle-lighting

Today the Saviour, promised long, is come. Emmanuel,
the Lord is with us. Amen.

The Saviour comes among us and is here. Emmanuel,
the Lord is with us. Amen.

Light the Christ candle.

His light shines in darkness that is about us. Emmanuel,
the Lord is with us. Amen.

Blessed are you, Lord our God,
for in your deep love for us
you have shared in our humanity
that we might share in your glory.
Help us to make room in our lives for you each day.
Let us be aware of you and of your coming to us.
May we know that we live in you as you live in us.
Blessed are you Father, Son and Holy Spirit.

Reading
Luke 2:1–14 or John 1:1–14

Hymn
Hark, the herald-angels sing *(first verse and refrain)*

Special intention – in the light of God

May we make room with the innkeeper
and know the joy of the shepherds,
the message of the angels,
the seeking of the wise men,
the bliss of Mary,
the presence of the Christ-child:
and may we rejoice in the Word made flesh
dwelling among us.

Closing prayer

O holy Child of Bethlehem,
descend to us we pray,
cast out our sin, and enter in;
be born in us today.

Extinguish candle.

The Epiphany

The Epiphany

Affirmation of God's presence

Affirmation

We celebrate today that Jesus is revealed to the wise men, who were not Jews, and so we rejoice in Jesus being revealed to all peoples.

Invitation to worship

God reveals himself to us. We are in the light and love of the Lord, Father, Son and Holy Spirit.

The Lord is here.
His Spirit is with us.

May Christ the daystar dawn in our hearts
and triumph over the shades of night.
Common Worship, Daily Prayer p.108

Hymn

O worship the Lord in the beauty of holiness

If possible have a star on a pole to lead the procession into church. Let children carry in the figures of the three wise men. Have three children dressed as wise men with their gifts and five other children to carry the Advent and Christmas candles. They will all go to their seats or stand in silence until the candle-lighting.

Silence

Candle-lighting

The people who walked in darkness have seen a great light. They lived in a land of shadows, but now light is shining upon them. You have given them great joy, O Lord; you have made them happy.
Isaiah 9:2, 3

Have five people light the candles, speaking the sentences as they do so.
Jesus, Word made flesh dwelling among us,
come, lighten our darkness. *First candle is lit*

Jesus born of the Blessed Virgin Mary,
come, lighten our darkness. *Second candle is lit*

Jesus adored by the wise men,
come, lighten our darkness. *Third candle is lit*

Jesus revealed to the world,
come, lighten our darkness. *Fourth candle is lit*

Jesus here and with us now,
come, lighten our darkness. *Central candle is lit*

The Word was made flesh and dwelt among us and we beheld his glory, as the glory of the only son of the Father full of grace and truth.
John 1:14

Blessed are you Lord our God for you have called us out of darkness to be children of light. The bright light of your presence scatters the darkness within us and is a lantern to our paths. Bless these lights that they may remind us of the light of your presence among us and your love for us all: through him who is the Light of the World, Jesus Christ our Lord. **Amen.**

Silence

Ministry of the Word

Reading
Isaiah 60:1–6, 19

Hymn
Earth has many a noble city

The Gospel
Matthew 2:1–12

Hymn

We three kings of Orient are

During the chorus after verse one the star will be placed behind the crib.

Sermon

Prayer

O God, who brought wise men to Jesus by the guiding of a star, bring us to know and to love your Son, Jesus Christ our Lord. **Amen.**

We remember before you, O God, all who seek your presence,
all who search for the truth,
all who look for meaning and who desire to know you.
We ask your blessing upon all who are growing in faith and love.
Guide and go with all pilgrim peoples,
especially those on their way to Bethlehem or Jerusalem.
Guide us, O Lord, in all our journeys throughout this life.
We pray for those who are new to our church or community.
Light of Christ,
shine in our lives.

During verse two have the gold-bearing figure placed at the crib and the child dressed as the gold bearer should come to the crib.

Prayer

God, giver of all good gifts,
as we remember the wise man bringing gold, we thank you for all that you have given to us and for your generous love.
We pray for the rich and the comfortable, all who have plenty of this world's goods: may they know that all things come from you and their lives are a gift from you. May the riches they have be put to good use for the benefit of the world.
We remember before you all who suffer from poverty, the world poor, the homeless and the hungry.
We ask your blessing upon all who feel their talents and gifts are not being used.
Light of Christ,
shine in our lives.

During verse three have the incense-bearing figure placed at the crib and the child dressed as the incense bearer should come to the crib.

Prayer

God, Holy and Almighty One, as we remember the wise man bringing incense, we come to love and adore you. Bless us in our worship and help us to know your abiding presence and love.
We give thanks for all who come to you in worship and in wonder, all that are aware of awe or mystery in their lives.
We ask your blessing upon all leaders of worship, choirs and organists, upon all who give us a sense of wonder and beauty.
Light of Christ,
shine in our lives.

During verse four have the myrrh-bearing figure placed at the crib and the child dressed as the myrrh bearer should come to the crib.

Prayer

God, as we remember the wise man bringing myrrh,
we rejoice that you sent your Son into the world for us and for our salvation. He is our Healer and our Saviour.
We remember that he suffered and died for us and for our redemption.
We come with all who are in pain or sorrow, we remember those whose sickness finds no cure, the permanently ill and those with a short time to live.
We ask your blessing upon all doctors and nurses and any who are involved in relieving pain and in healing.
Light of Christ,
shine in our lives.

At verse five the children dressed as wise men should kneel before the Christ child at the crib. During the final chorus let the children stand up and bow toward the Christ child and then go dancing back to their places.

Prayer

Lord we worship and adore you.
We offer you our joys and sorrows, our sickness and health, our riches and our poverty.

We remember all who have enriched our lives by their goodness.
We ask your blessing upon our homes and loved ones.
We pray for loved ones who are now departed from us and are in the fullness of your kingdom.
Merciful Father,
accept these prayers for the sake of your Son, our Saviour Jesus Christ. Amen.

O God, who by the leading of a star brought the wise men to Bethlehem, guide us through each day and night on our journey of faith.
Lord, give us the courage to persevere that we are not put off in our search for you.
May we witness to your gospel and rejoice in your glory.
May we seek to do your will until we enter the fullness of your kingdom.
We ask this in the name of him who came and lived among us, Jesus Christ our Lord.
Amen.

Silence

Hymn
As with gladness men of old

Response

Creed

Confession

Collect
O God, who by the leading of a star
manifested your only Son to the peoples of the earth:
mercifully grant that we,
who know you now by faith,
may behold your glory face to face;
through Jesus Christ our Lord.
Amen.

Common Worship Collect for Epiphany.

The Lord's Prayer

Silence

Hymn
Christ is the world's true light

Blessing

Let the bright light of Christ enlighten your heart,
shine in your life and direct your journeying.
Rejoice, for the light of Christ disperses the darkness of this world,
and the blessing of God Almighty,
the Father, the Son and the Holy Spirit be upon you
and your loved ones now and always.
Amen.

The wise men

Begin in the dark. If the room is not dark, close your eyes.

Welcome the light

The people who walked in darkness have seen a great light; they who lived in a land of deep darkness, on them the light has shined.

Isaiah 9:2

Jesus, Word made flesh dwelling among us,
come, lighten our darkness.

Jesus, born of the Blessed Virgin Mary,
come, lighten our darkness.

Jesus, adored by the wise men,
come, lighten our darkness.

Jesus, revealed to the world,
come, lighten our darkness.

Candle-lighting

Jesus here and with us now,
come, lighten our darkness.

Jesus Christ is the Light of the World.
A light that no darkness can extinguish.

Light the candle.

Blessed are you, O Lord God, who by the leading of a star brought the wise men to come before Jesus. Through him, who is our Saviour, you reveal your love and light to the whole world. In our seeking, guide us that we may come before you, that we may come to know you, to love you and to worship you this day and always. Blessed are you Father, Son and Holy Spirit.

Lord God, to live without you is to walk in the darkness:
to live in awareness of you is to live in the light.
Help us to know and to reveal your love
and your light through Jesus Christ our Lord.
Amen.

Reading
Matthew 2:1–12

Hymn
As with gladness men of old *(first verse)*

Special intention – in the light of God

Blessed be God, who by the leading of a star brought the wise men to Christ the King.
The Word has become flesh
and now lives among us.

Blessed be God, who is the God of all the nations.
The Word has become flesh
and now lives among us.

Blessed be God, who comes to all peoples, in all places and all the time.
The Word has become flesh
and now lives among us.

Christ was proclaimed by the angels.
The Word has become flesh
and now lives among us.

Christ was worshipped by the shepherds.
The Word has become flesh
and now lives among us.

Christ was adored by the wise men.
The Word has become flesh
and now lives among us.

Christ is worshipped throughout the world.
The Word has become flesh
and now lives among us.

Closing prayer

Lord, we come to the light of your presence and to your love.
Lord, whom we sought in the sky, you are found here among us.
Lord, who remained long hidden from sight,
you are found in an infant.
Today we rejoice, for heaven has come to earth:
earth is taken up into heaven.
God is found in human flesh and our humanity is taken up into God.
He whom the universe could not contain is found in a tiny child.
We come and adore with those who seek you.
We acknowledge you as our King and our God.
We know you have shared in our sorrows to redeem us.
We offer ourselves to you who came down to raise us up.
We adore you, Christ our Lord.

Extinguish candle.

The Baptism of our Lord

Today you might like to renew your baptismal vows and say the creed.

Begin in the dark. If the room is not dark, close your eyes.

Welcome the light

In those days Jesus came from Nazareth of Galilee and was baptised by John in the Jordan.

Mark 1:9

We give thanks for the baptism of Jesus by John in the river Jordan. We rejoice that God's voice was heard affirming his Son and that the Holy Spirit was known to descend upon Jesus. Rejoice, for we are always immersed in the presence of God, Father, Son and Holy Spirit. We abide in him as he abides in us. In the name of the Father, and of the Son and of the Holy Spirit.
Amen.

The Lord is here:
his Spirit is with us.

Candle-lighting

Jesus Christ is the Light of the World.
A light that no darkness can extinguish.

Light the candle.

O Lord Jesus, you came down to dwell among us,
you were fully immersed in our humanity.
you were immersed in the waters of the Jordan
as you are in our earthly life.
As the waters flowed all around you,
may we know that that you are for ever about us.

As we are baptised in your Name,
may we know that we dwell in you and that you are in us.
Blessed are you, Lord Jesus Christ, with the Father and the Holy Spirit, One God now and for ever.
Amen.

Reading
Matthew 3:13–17

Hymn
Songs of thankfulness and praise *(second verse)*

Renew your baptismal vows and say the creed at this point, if appropriate.

Special intention – in the light of God

We give thanks for the gift of water in Creation,
for rain, for rivers and seas, for pools and for oceans,
for the power of water to cleanse and refresh us,
for the life-giving properties of water,
for Jesus Christ immersed in the waters of the Jordan;
that our Lord is one with us and we dwell in him.
We rejoice in our own baptism
and that we are immersed in the Father, the Son and the Holy Spirit.

Closing prayer

God to enfold me,
God to surround me,
God in my speaking,
God in my thinking.
God in my sleeping,
God in my waking,
God in my watching,
God in my hoping.
God in my life,
God in my lips,
God in my soul,
God in my heart.

God in my sufficing,
God in my slumber,
God in mine ever-living soul,
God in mine eternity.
Carmina Gadelica III

Extinguish candle.

Immersed in God

Affirmation of God's presence

Affirmation

We come to give thanks for the Baptism of Jesus by John in the River Jordan. We rejoice that God's voice was heard affirming his Son and that the Holy Spirit was known to descend upon Jesus.

Invitation to worship

We are always immersed in the presence of God, Father, Son and Holy Spirit. Let us abide in him as he abides in us.

The Lord is here.
His Spirit is with us.

Hymn

Thou whose almighty word

Silence

Candle-lighting

Today have the candle-lighting near the font which is filled with water.

Have four people, with lighted tapers, in different corners of the church. Let a fifth person with a lighted taper stand in the centre of the church. (This can be more effective if the lights are left off until the candles are lit.)

Let one person begin by saying, 'We rejoice in the presence,' and asking the congregation to respond, **'of Father, Son and Holy Spirit'**. In turn let the people with tapers light a single candle. After each one lights a candle they say, 'We rejoice in the presence' and the congregation responds, **'of Father, Son and Holy Spirit.'**

1. I light this candle in thanksgiving for God the Father, the creator of light.
   We rejoice in the presence
   of Father, Son and Holy Spirit.

2. I light this candle in thanksgiving for Jesus Christ the Light of the World.
   We rejoice in the presence
   of Father, Son and Holy Spirit.

3. I light this candle in thanksgiving for the Holy Spirit who enlightens us all.
   We rejoice in the presence
   of Father, Son and Holy Spirit.

4. I light this candle in thanksgiving for the glory of the Holy Trinity.
   We rejoice in the presence
   of Father, Son and Holy Spirit.

5. I light this candle in thanksgiving for Jesus baptised for us and our salvation.
   We rejoice in the presence
   of Father, Son and Holy Spirit.

This is a good day to use the 'Peruvian Gloria' after the candle-lighting or after the renewal of the baptismal vows.

After the Gospel reading the congregation can then renew their baptismal vows and have the opportunity to dip their finger in the water and sign themselves with the sign of the cross.

Silence

Ministry of the Word

Reading
Isaiah 65:17–25

Hymn
Spirit of God unseen as the wind

The Gospel
John 3:1–12

Sermon

Silence

Hymn
Christ, when for us you were baptised

Response

Renewal of baptismal vows

The Decision
In baptism, God calls us out of darkness into his marvellous light. To follow Christ means dying to sin and rising to new life with him. Therefore I ask:

Do you reject the devil and all rebellion against God?
I reject them.

Do you renounce the deceit and corruption of evil?
I renounce them.

Do you repent of the sins that separate us from God and neighbour?
I repent of them.

Do you turn to Christ as Saviour?
I turn to Christ.

Do you submit to Christ as Lord?
I submit to Christ.

Do you come to Christ, the way, the truth and the life?
I come to Christ.
Common Worship, Services and Prayers for the Church of England p.143

At this point the congregation can be invited to come to the font, dip their finger in the water and make the sign of the cross on their forehead. They can say: **I am signed with the cross for I belong to Christ.**

Creed

Do you believe and trust in God the Father,
source of all being and life, the one for whom we exist?
I believe and trust in him.

Do you believe and trust in God the Son,
who took our human nature,
died for us and rose again?
I believe and trust in him.

Do you believe and trust in God the Holy Spirit,
who gives life to the people of God
and makes Christ known in the world?
I believe and trust in him.

This is the faith of the Church.
This is our faith.
We believe and trust in one God,
Father, Son and Holy Spirit.

Common Worship, Services and Prayers for the Church of England p.143

Confession

Thanksgiving

Praise and thanks to you Lord our God
for you have created all things from the beginning.
Praise and thanks to you Lord Jesus Christ;
you lived among us and were baptised of John.
Blessed are you Holy Spirit of power and might,
you descend as the dove filling us with life.
Blessed are you holy and blessed Three,
in you we live and move and have our being.
Amen.

Intercessions

Holy God, holy and strong One, holy and Mighty One,
thank you for our baptism and that you enfold us in love:
may we know that we dwell in you and you are in us.
Bless, O Lord, all who are baptised, may they rejoice in your abiding love.

We remember before you our godchildren and our godparents and all who have been baptised in this place, all who are being prepared for baptism or confirmation at this time.
Give to them and all your Church the power to show that we are members of Christ, children of God and inheritors of the kingdom of heaven.
Lord, we believe in you:
we trust in you.

Lord of all power and might, let your peace be known among us.
We remember all involved in conflict, those not at peace with themselves or with others.
Lord, bless all who are suffering from captivity or tyranny.
We remember for all who are slaves to debt or caught up in poverty.
Lord, we believe in you:
we trust in you.

We ask your blessing upon those who have shared their lives and their faith with us and upon all who have been concerned with our well-being.
Protect and bless our families and our friends, our neighbourhood and our land and keep us in your peace.
Lord, we believe in you:
we trust in you.

Bless all who are feeling lonely or anxious, those who are ill, those who have been involved in an accident or suffered from violence.
Give courage and hope to all who have suffered spiritually, physically or mentally, and to those with memories that disturb or frighten them.
Mighty God, comfort those who have lost confidence in themselves or in others.
We remember the world-weary, weak, and the sad.
Lord, we believe in you:
we trust in you.

We ask your blessing upon all your faithful people; we remember especially loved ones who are departed from us.
May they rejoice in that greater awareness of Father, Son and Holy Spirit and may we rejoice with them as inheritors of the kingdom of heaven.
Merciful Father,
accept these prayers for the sake of your Son,
our Saviour Jesus Christ.
Amen.

Collect

Eternal Father,
who at the baptism of Jesus
revealed him to be your Son,
anointing him with the Holy Spirit:
grant to us, who are born again by water and the Spirit,
that we may be faithful to our calling as your adopted children;
through Jesus Christ our Lord.

Common Worship Collect for The Baptism of Christ

The Lord's Prayer

Silence

Hymn

Spirit of the living God, fall afresh on me (Iverson)

Blessing

God, the Creator, uphold you.
Christ, the Redeemer, enfold you.
The Holy Spirit, the Comforter, guide you,
and the blessing of God Almighty,
the Father, the Son and the Holy Spirit be upon you
and remain with you always.
Amen.

Celebrating the water made wine

Affirmation of God's presence

Affirmation

Today we celebrate the first miracle of Jesus at the wedding feast at Cana when he turned the water into wine. We celebrate the revealing of the power of Jesus to change our lives.

Invitation to worship

We rejoice in Christ's power to transform our lives and to fill our emptiness with the riches of his glory.

The Lord is here.
His Spirit is with us.

Hymn

New every morning is the love

Silence

Candle-lighting

Have five people light the candles, speaking the sentences as they do so.

Holy God, holy and Strong One, in our emptiness we come to be filled by you. *First candle is lit.*
The Lord is my light and my salvation.

Holy God, holy and Strong One, in our darkness we come to your light. *Second candle is lit.*
The Lord is my light and my salvation.

Holy God, holy and Strong One, in our troubles we come to your love. *Third candle is lit.*
The Lord is my light and my salvation.

Holy God, holy and Strong One, in illness we come for your healing.
Fourth candle is lit.
The Lord is my light and my salvation.

Holy God, holy and Strong One, in need we come to your salvation.
Fifth candle is lit.
The Lord is my light and my salvation.

Prayer
Lord you know our needs before we ask and are always more ready to give than we desire or deserve. We come to you for healing renewal and for the fullness of life eternal. **Amen.**

Silence

Ministry of the Word

Reading
1 Kings 17:8–16

Hymn
Jesus the Lord said, 'I am the bread'

The Gospel
John 2:1–11

Sermon

Silence

Hymn
Joy to the world

Response

Creed

Confession

Thanksgiving

Lord Jesus, we give thanks that you come to share in our joys and in our sorrows. We rejoice that you bring your strength to our weakness, your presence to our emptiness. We give thanks that in you we are transformed into your likeness and can share in your glory.

Intercessions

Lord, at the wedding of Cana,
you transformed common water into wine,
come and change us that we may know you and your love:
as you dear Lord have taken on our humanity
may we now partake of your Divinity.
Good Lord transform us
that we may reveal your glory.

Bless your Church as it seeks to reveal your glory in the world.
We remember especially all priests, pastors and ministers and all your faithful people in their obedience and witness to you.
We ask your blessing upon all that are preparing for marriage and all who are newly married. We pray for those saving to get married and all who feel that they cannot afford to marry.
Good Lord transform us
that we may reveal your glory.

Remember before you all that are discovering a newness in their love for each other.
We pray for marriages that have run into difficulties, for those who are running out of resources, those in debt and those having homes repossessed.
For all who feel betrayed in their love, for those seeking a divorce at this time.
We ask your blessing upon marriage guidance councils and all who seek to support family life.
Good Lord transform us
that we may reveal your glory.

Lord that your presence may transform our homes: that our homes may be centres of love, joy and peace.
We remember before you friends and loved ones and all who have transformed our lives by their goodness.
We ask that in our communities we may share and help to meet each other's needs.
We pray for those areas of darkness and deprivation within our communities.
Good Lord transform us
that we may reveal your glory.

We remember all who have run out of resources, the hungry and thirsty peoples of our world.
We ask your blessing upon the exhausted, the world-weary and all who can no longer cope on their own, upon all who are struggling to provide for their families and their basic needs.
We remember all who are in trouble or in sickness, especially . . .
Good Lord transform us
that we may reveal your glory.

We rejoice that in you the best is yet to come.
We give thanks for all who have entered into the glory of your kingdom.
We pray for loved ones departed from our sight, especially . . .
Merciful Father,
accept these prayers for the sake of your Son our Saviour Jesus Christ. Amen.

Collect

Almighty God,
whose Son revealed in signs and miracles
the wonder of your saving presence:
renew your people with your heavenly grace,
and in all our weakness
sustain us with your mighty power;
through Jesus Christ our Lord.

Common Worship Collect for the Third Sunday of Epiphany

The Lord's Prayer

Silence

Hymn
How sweet the name of Jesus sounds

Blessing

The love of the Lord Jesus fill you with joy and newness of life,
the Lord Jesus bring you to the fullness of his glory,
the Lord Jesus transform your days by his presence,
and the blessing of God Almighty,
the Father, the Son and the Holy Spirit
be upon you and your loved ones now and always.
Amen.

The transforming power of Christ

Begin in the dark. If the room is not dark, close your eyes.

Welcome the light

Today we celebrate the first miracle of Jesus at the wedding feast in Cana when he turned the water into wine. We celebrate the revealing of the power of Jesus to change our lives. We rejoice in Christ's power to transform us and to fill our emptiness with the riches of his glory.
The Lord is here:
his Spirit is with us.

He gives power to the faint, and strengthens the powerless. Those who wait on the Lord shall renew their strength, they shall mount up with wings like eagles, they shall run and not be weary, they shall walk and not faint.

Isaiah 40:29, 31

Lord, you know our needs before we ask and are always more ready to give than we desire or deserve. We come to you for healing, for renewal and for the fullness of life eternal.
Amen.

Candle-lighting

Jesus Christ is the Light of the world.
A light that no darkness can extinguish.

Light the candle.

Blessed are you, Lord our God; you have made us in your image, and restored that image through your Son, Christ our Lord. You fill our emptiness with your presence, you transform our weakness by your power, you make what is common into that which is precious.

As Christ changed the water into wine, you renew our lives each day.
Blessed are you Father, Son and Holy Spirit.

Reading
John 2:1–11

Hymn
New every morning is the love

Special intention – in the light of God

Holy God, holy and Strong One, in our emptiness we come to be filled by you.
The Lord is my light and my salvation.

Holy God, holy and Strong One, in our darkness we come to your light.
The Lord is my light and my salvation.

Holy God, holy and Strong One, in our troubles we come to your love.
The Lord is my light and my salvation.

Holy God, holy and Strong One, in illness we come for your healing.
The Lord is my light and my salvation.

Holy God, holy and Strong One, in need we come to your salvation.
The Lord is my light and my salvation.

Closing prayer

Lord, at the wedding of Cana,
you transformed common water into wine –
come and change us, that we may know you and your love:
as you, dear Lord, have taken on our humanity
may we now partake of your Divinity.
Good Lord, transform us that we may reveal your glory.

Extinguish candle.

The mission of the Church

Affirmation of God's presence

Affirmation

God has called us to know him and to love him. Those whom God calls he sends. God wants to reveal himself to others through us and our way of life.

Invitation to worship

We are in the presence of God the Father, Son and Holy Spirit: we live in his light and are for ever in his love. Come and give your love to him.

The Lord is here.
His Spirit is with us.

Hymn

I, the Lord of sea and sky

Silence

Candle-lighting

Today we light our five candles to rejoice that Jesus is ever present and gives himself to us. He desires us to share in his love for the world.

Have five different people light the candles, speaking the sentences as they do so.

Jesus, Light of the World, I give myself to you. *First candle is lit.*

Jesus, our loving Lord, I give myself to you. *Second candle is lit.*

Jesus, our Friend and Saviour, I give myself to you. *Third candle is lit.*

Jesus as you give yourself for us, I give myself to you.
Fourth candle is lit.

Jesus, the Son of God and Son of man, I give myself to you.
Fifth candle is lit.

All: **Jesus you call us to work with you: we give our lives to you.**

Prayer

Jesus Christ, Light of the World, you reveal yourself to your disciples. Open our ears to your call and help us to be faithful and serve you all our days. **Amen.**

Silence

Ministry of the Word

Reading

Isaiah 6:1–8

Hymn

We have a gospel to proclaim

The Gospel

Matthew 28:16–20

Sermon

Silence

Hymn

Firmly I believe and truly

Response

Creed

Confession

Thanksgiving

Blessed are you, Lord our God, for you have called us to know you and to abide with you. You have called us to love you and to tell of you. Blessed are you Father, Son and Holy Spirit for you have called us into life and life eternal. Blessed be God for ever.

Intercessions

Father we ask your blessing upon the Church, that it may grow in love for you, that it may grow in holiness, that it may grow in size. We remember before you all who reach out in mission to tell of your love and your saving power. Lord guide all preachers of the word and teachers of the faith, all who witness by their daily lives and example. May we all share in bringing others to you and in revealing you to others.
Lord, as you call us,
fill us with your love.

Lord God, we pray for all who are being exploited by others. We remember the poor and the homeless and we ask your blessing upon all who are caring for refugees and deprived peoples. We pray for all who lack any moral or spiritual guidance and who are being led astray by people around them.
Lord, as you call us,
fill us with your love.

We give thanks for those who taught us the faith and who set us an example by their lives. We ask your blessing upon our homes, our loved ones and all who have cared for us. We pray for all who suffer from neglect, violence or a lack of love.
Lord, as you call us,
fill us with your love.

God, in you is our peace and our hope. We remember in your presence all ill and suffering people. We pray especially for any who feel confused by life and who are not able to cope. We pray for all who are caught up in drug abuse or in vice. May all who deal with the troubled and distressed help to bring your peace and love to their lives.
Lord, as you call us,
fill us with your love.

We give thanks for your redeeming love and for the gift of life eternal.
We ask your blessing on our loved ones departed and commend them, this world and ourselves to your unfailing love.
Merciful Father,
accept these prayers for the sake of your Son, our Saviour Jesus Christ. Amen.

Collect

God our creator, who in the beginning
commanded the light to shine out of darkness:
we pray that the light of the glorious gospel of Christ
may dispel the darkness of ignorance and unbelief,
shine into the hearts of all your people,
and reveal the knowledge of your glory
in the face of Jesus Christ your Son our Lord.

Common Worship Collect for the Fourth Sunday of Epiphany

The Lord's Prayer

Silence

Hymn

Forth in thy name, O Lord, I go

Blessing

The love of the Father empower you,
the light of the Saviour radiate from you,
the leading of the Spirit guide you
and the blessing of God Almighty,
the Father, the Son and the Holy Spirit
be upon you now and for evermore.
Amen.

Working with Christ

Begin in the dark. If the room is not dark, close your eyes.

Welcome the light

Arise, shine, for your light has come, and the glory of the Lord is risen upon you. For darkness shall cover the earth, and thick darkness the peoples; but the glory of the Lord will arise upon you, and his glory will appear over you. Nations shall come to you light, and kings to the brightness of your dawn.

Isaiah 60:1–3

The light which the wise men followed was found in the Christ child.
The Lord is our light and our salvation.

Candle-lighting

Jesus Christ is the Light of the world.
A light that no darkness can extinguish.

Light the candle.

Blessed are you, Lord our God, for you have called us to know you and to walk in your light. You have called us to love you and to reveal your light in our lives and to the world. Blessed are you, Father, Son and Holy Spirit, for you have called us into life and life eternal. Blessed be God for ever.

Readings

Matthew 28:16–20; Matthew 5:14–16

Hymn

I, the Lord of sea and sky

Set our hearts on fire with love for you, O Christ,
that in its flame we may love you,
with all our heart,

with all our mind,
with all our soul,
and with all our strength,
and our neighbour as ourselves,
so that, in keeping your commandments,
we may glorify you, the giver of all good gifts.
Kontakion for Love, Eastern Orthodox Church

Special intention – in the light of God

In your coming, O Christ, the darkness is conquered.
Jesus, Light of the World, I give myself to you.

you Lord, in your light, reveal to us your love.
Jesus, Light of the World, I give myself to you.

you, Lord, are the Light to lighten all the nations.
Jesus, Light of the World, I give myself to you.

you, Lord, ask us to let our light shine in the world.
Jesus, Light of the World, I give myself to you.

you, Lord, have called us to witness to you.
Jesus, Light of the World, I give myself to you.

May the world know that we dwell in you and you in us.

Closing prayer

Arise, shine; for your light has come,
and the glory of the Lord has risen upon you.
Arise, shine; for your light has come.

For darkness shall cover the earth, and thick darkness the peoples; but the Lord will arise upon you, and his glory will appear over you.
Arise, shine; for your light has come.

Nations shall come to your light, and kings to the brightness of your dawn.
Arise, shine; for your light has come.

Isaiah 60:1-3

Extinguish candle.

Candlemas

2 February

The Lord is my light

If possible, everyone should be given a candle before starting.

Begin in the dark. If the room is not dark, close your eyes.

The darkness represents our world and our lives without Christ.

In the darkness ask all present to quietly invite Jesus the Light of the World into their lives.

Our bright shining candles are a sign of the divine splendour of the one who comes to expel the dark shadows of evil and to make the whole universe radiant with the brilliance of his eternal light. Our candles also show how bright our souls should be when we go to meet Christ.

The God-bearer, the most pure Virgin, carried the true Light in her arms and brought him to help those who lay in darkness. We too should carry a light for all to see and reflect the radiance of the true light as we hasten to meet him.

Indeed, this is the mystery we celebrate today: the light has come and has shone upon a world enveloped in shadows; the Dayspring from on high has visited us and given light to those who lived in darkness. This, then, is our feast, and we join in procession with lighted candles to reveal the light that has shone upon us and the glory that is yet to come to us through him. So let us hasten all together to meet our God.

The true light has come, the light that enlightens everyone who is born into this world. Let all of us be enlightened and made radiant by this light. Let all of us share in its splendour, and be so filled with it that no one remains in the darkness. Let us be shining ourselves as we go together to meet and to receive with the aged Simeon the light whose brilliance is eternal.

Sophronius of Jerusalem 6th–7th century

Welcome the light

The Lord is my light and my salvation; whom shall I fear?
The Lord is my light and my salvation.

The Lord is the stronghold of my life; of whom shall I be afraid?
The Lord is my light and my salvation.

Glory be to the Father, and to the Son, and to the Holy Spirit.
The Lord is my light and my salvation.

Psalm 27:1, 2

Candle-lighting

May Christ the Daystar dawn in our hearts
and triumph over the shades of night.

Jesus Christ is the Light of the World.
A light that no darkness can extinguish.

Light the candle.

Blessed are you, Lord God; to you be all praise and glory for ever and ever, for you are our light and our salvation. You created light out of darkness and have revealed your light and love in our lives through the birth of your Son, our Lord Jesus Christ. Blessed are you, Father, Son and Holy Spirit, one God for ever and ever.

If possible everyone present lights a candle or a taper from the lit candle and declares: **The Lord is my light and my salvation.**

Reading
Luke 2:22–40

Hymn
Christ, whose glory fills the skies

Special intention – in the light of God

Come, Lord of light:
Lighten our darkness;
Lighten our lives with your love;
Lighten our homes with your presence;
Lighten this world with your peace.
Come, Lord of Light, be known to be among us.

Closing prayer

Lord, as we move from here we are still in your presence,
your light is with us and before us.
Your light leads us and guides us.
In your light we live and move and have our being.
your light will help us to banish the deeds of darkness.
As we extinguish this light, we rejoice that we dwell in your Light
and we are in your presence always.

Stay for a while rejoicing in the light of Christ.

Extinguish the candle.

The presentation of Christ in the temple

Affirmation of God's presence

Affirmation

Today is the festival of the presentation of Christ in the Temple; it was known earlier as the festival of the purification of Mary. It is probably best known simply as Candlemas. There is a sense in which the lighting of the candles throughout the Advent, Christmas and Epiphany season now reach their climax. The forty days of Christmas close with Candlemas. The year is coming out of darkness and the days are lengthening. After today, we turn towards the season of Lent and look forward to Easter. As a symbol of this movement, we will process to the door of the church at the end of the service and there extinguish our candles.

It is our joy to welcome Christ as did Simeon and Anna: to welcome him as 'a light to lighten the nations of the world and the glory of his people Israel'. Let us rejoice in the Light of Christ that has come into our world.

Invitation to worship

We are in the light, the love and the glory of the Lord, Father, Son and Holy Spirit.

The Lord is here.
His Spirit is with us.

Hymn

Father, we adore you

Silence

Candle-lighting

If possible have a candle for everyone to light during the service or at least one for a representative from each family.

Have five people come from different areas of the church for the candle-lighting. Begin by telling the congregation the response to 'Christ as our Light,' is '**illumine and guide us**.'

As the five people light the candles each has a sentence to say:
Jesus Christ is the Light of all the peoples of world.
Christ as our Light,
illumine and guide us.

Jesus Christ is the Light that scatters the darkness.
Christ as our Light,
illumine and guide us.

Jesus Christ is the Light to show us the way to the Father.
Christ as our Light,
illumine and guide us.

Jesus Christ is the Light that leads us to eternal life.
Christ as our Light,
illumine and guide us.

The Good News is Jesus the Light of the World is with us now.
Christ as our Light,
illumine and guide us.

Hymn

We are marching in the light of God

Let everyone receive a light from the main candles or from each other as the hymn is sung.

Prayer after the hymn

Blessed are you Lord our God for you have called us out of darkness to share in your light. The bright light of Christ scatters the darkness from within us and is a lantern to our path. Bless these lights that we

carry that they may remind us of your presence and of your saving love revealed through Christ our Lord.
Christ as our Light,
illumine and guide us.

Silence

Ministry of the Word

Reading
1 Samuel 1:20–28

Hymn
Christ is the world's light

The Gospel
Luke 2:22–40

Sermon

Silence

Hymn
Lord, the light of your love is shining

Response

Creed

Confession

Thanksgiving
Blessed are you Lord our God.
We give you thanks and praise for the creation of the light that gives life to the world.
We rejoice in Christ our Lord who brings light to our darkness.
We praise you for the light of Spirit, who inspires and guides us.
Today we give you thanks for the presentation of Christ in the Temple, for the vision of Simeon,

for the faith of Anna,
for the steadfastness of Joseph,
for the courage of Mary, as she was told she would suffer with her Son.
Above all, we thank you that in Christ we triumph over darkness and death.
Blessed are you Father, Son and Holy Spirit, one God for ever and ever.
Amen.

Intercessions

By the mystery of the Word made flesh, Lord,
make yourself known to us.

By your coming as Christ the Light of the World, Lord,
make yourself known to us.

By your birth in Bethlehem, Lord,
make yourself known to us.

By your revealing to the shepherds and wise men, Lord,
make yourself known to us.

By your baptism, with the voice from the cloud and the descending dove, Lord,
make yourself known to us.

By your presence at the wedding at Cana and your changing water into wine, Lord,
make yourself known to us.

By your proclaiming of the Good News, Lord,
make yourself known to us.

God of light and love, we remember before you all who seek to proclaim the Good News. We ask your blessing upon all ministers of the word and the sacraments, upon all who teach and preach in your name. We pray for all who are striving to bring the Light of Christ to darkened lives.
Light of God,
shine upon us.

We remember all who live in darkness and in fear. We pray for the persecuted and the homeless, for all who are captives or suffer from war or terrorism. We ask your blessing upon all who are anxious for their lives.
Light of God,
shine upon us.

We remember for all who suffer from blindness or impairment of their sight. We ask you to bless all who seek to relieve their suffering and to restore sight. We pray for any who have lost vision of you and your love.
Light of God,
shine upon us.

We remember all who are in the valley of the shadow of death and all who have passed beyond it to light and life eternal. We pray for our loved ones departed from us. May we all come to rejoice in the fullness of your kingdom.
Merciful Father,
accept these prayers for the sake of your Son, our Saviour Jesus Christ.
Amen.

Collect

Almighty Father,
whose Son Jesus Christ was presented in the Temple
and acclaimed the glory of Israel
and the light of the nations:
grant that in him we may be presented to you
and in the world may reflect his glory:
through Jesus Christ our Lord,
who is alive and reigns with you and the Holy Spirit,
one God, now and for ever.
Amen.

The Alternative Service Book 1980

The Lord's Prayer

Silence

Hymn
The Nunc dimittis *or* Faithful vigil ended

During the hymn there is a procession to the door.

Here we turn from our celebration of Christ's coming into the world and towards Lent and Easter: turning from his birth to his passion and resurrection. We remember that he came among us and that he shares in our joys and sorrows. May we, who now extinguish these candles, let the light of Christ shine in our hearts and lives and bring his light to the world.

The candles are extinguished.

Blessing

The Lord Jesus, give light to your eyes,
give light to your mind,
give light to your heart,
give light to your hands,
give light to your whole life,
that you may witness to him and live for him, today and for ever,
and the blessing of God Almighty,
the Father, the Son and the Holy Spirit
be upon you and remain with you always.
Amen.

Lent

Ash Wednesday

Affirmation of God's presence

Affirmation

Welcome to this special service for Ash Wednesday. The use of ashes on this day is to help us to put our lives into proper focus. We affirm in the presence of God that we come from God; that we are created out of his love and that we depend upon him. At the same time we acknowledge our mortality that we are of the dust of the earth and to that dust we will return.

Lent is a time for reviewing our life. We are invited to look at the way we live and who we think we truly are. The imposition of ashes reminds us that our time on earth is limited as are the resources of the earth. It makes us ask what we are doing with our lives: by what priorities do we live, or do we just drift? Lent presents us with a challenge, a time to redirect and refocus our lives. Let the imposition of ashes be a challenge to your way of thinking and acting.

In the Old Testament we are told that we are made of the dust of the earth and to dust we shall return (Genesis 3:19). But this is only half of the picture for we are made out of the love of God and it is to that love we shall return: hence the signing of the cross. In the Old Testament ashes were a symbol of sorrow for sin and our failure to live up to our potential. Ashes are a sign of our desire to make amends, to turn our life around, of our repentance, our once more turning to God and his love.

Lent is a time when those who were being prepared for baptism were having their faith extended: a time when those who were seeking restoration into the Church were discovering forgiveness and renewal.

I invite you to begin this Lent by receiving the imposition of ashes, with a commitment to the service of God through prayer, almsgiving and fasting. May your growth in faith bring you to know him and to the fullness of eternal life.

Invitation to worship

We are in the presence, in the love and in the power of God, Father, Son and Holy Spirit. **Amen.**

The Lord is here.
His Spirit is with us.

Hymn
I, the Lord of sea and sky

Silence

Ministry of the Word

Old Testament
Genesis 3:17–19 or Joel 2:1, 2, 12–17

Hymn
O for a heart to praise my God

The Gospel
Matthew 6:1–6, 16–21

Sermon

Silence

Hymn
Dear Lord and Father

Response

Thanksgiving
Blessed are you Lord our God, for though you created us from the dust of the earth you created us by your love for your love. You have breathed your life-giving Spirit into us. We thank you for this time of repentance, renewal and amendment of life. We rejoice in your gift of forgiveness and your love as revealed in Jesus Christ our Lord. Praise and thanks to you Father, Son and Holy Spirit, one God now and for ever.

Creed

Litany

God the Father,
have mercy on us.

God the Son,
have mercy on us.

God the Holy Spirit,
have mercy on us.

Holy, blessed and glorious Trinity,
have mercy on us.

Give us true repentance;
forgive us our sins of negligence and ignorance
and our deliberate sins;
and grant us the grace of your Holy Spirit
to amend our lives according to your holy word.
Holy God,
holy and strong,
holy and immortal,
have mercy upon us.

Sections I and VII from The Litany in Common Worship Daily Prayer p.400 and 403

Confession

Make us a clean heart, O God,
and renew a right spirit within us.

The Imposition of Ashes

As a sign of the spirit of repentance with which we shall keep this season of preparation for Easter, I invite you to receive on your head in ash the sign of the cross, the symbol of the love of God in salvation.

Almighty God,
you created us out of your love, and from the dust of the earth.
Let these ashes be a sign of our turning to you
and a symbol of our mortality.
May we remember that we come from you
and that by your love alone we are given eternal life;
through Jesus Christ our Lord and Saviour.

In the name of Jesus Christ our Saviour, I invite you to receive on your head the sign of the cross.
Those who desire to receive the imposition of ashes now come forward.
At each signing is said:
Remember that you are but dust and to dust you shall return.
Turn away from sin and be faithful to Christ.

The Absolution

Intercessions

We remember before you, O Lord,
all who are seeking to keep a Holy Lent,
all who are amending their lives,
all who are dedicating themselves in your service.
Lord, hear us.
Lord, mercifully hear us.

We remember before you, O Lord,
all who are being prepared for baptism or confirmation,
all who are seeking to grow in the faith,
all who are searching for meaning and purpose.
Lord, hear us.
Lord, mercifully hear us.

We remember before you, O Lord,
all who are struggling with sin,
all who are caught up in addiction, vice or violence,
all who suffer because of loved one's sin.
Lord, hear us.
Lord, mercifully hear us.
We remember before you, O Lord,

all who are suffering for their faith,
all who are ill or afflicted,
all who are poor and homeless.
Lord, hear us.
Lord, mercifully hear us.

We remember before you, O Lord, that we are dust of the earth,
but to you we shall return,
and we ask your blessing upon our loved ones departed from us.
Merciful Father,
accept these prayers for the sake of your Son, Jesus Christ our Lord.
Amen.

Collect

Almighty and everlasting God,
you hate nothing that you have made
and forgive the sins of all those who are penitent:
create and make in us new and contrite hearts
that we, worthily lamenting our sins
and acknowledging our wretchedness,
may receive from you, the God of all mercy,
perfect remission and forgiveness;
through Jesus Christ our Lord.

Common Worship Collect for Ash Wednesday

The Lord's Prayer

Silence

Hymn

O Jesus, I have promised

Blessing

God give you grace to keep a holy Lent,
to turn away from sin and grow in holiness,
to be faithful to him in all that you say and do:
and the blessing of God Almighty,
the Father, the Son and the Holy Spirit
be upon you and your loved ones, now and for evermore.
Amen.

Lent 1
Temptations

Affirmation of God's presence

Affirmation

As we remember the temptations of Jesus in the wilderness, we acknowledge that we are all tempted and we often fail to be the people God has called us to be, or do what God has called us to do. By giving in to temptation we live a life that is below what God created us to live. We affirm today that God is with us and gives us strength to fight against evil and choose what is right.

Invitation to worship

We are in the presence, power and the forgiveness of God, Father, Son and Holy Spirit.

The Lord is here.
His Spirit is with us.

Hymn

He who would valiant be

Silence

Litany

God the Father,
have mercy upon us.

God the Son,
have mercy upon us.

God the Holy Spirit,
have mercy upon us.

Holy and blessed Trinity,
have mercy upon us.

Jesus tempted as we are,
hear us and help us.

Jesus in your victory over evil,
hear us and help us.

Jesus unwilling to compromise,
hear us and help us.

Jesus determined to serve God,
hear us and help us.

Silence

Ministry of the Word

Old Testament
Genesis 3:1–7

Hymn
Forty days and forty nights

The Gospel
Matthew 4:1–11

Sermon

Silence

Hymn
Lord of our life, and God of our salvation

Response

Creed

Confession

Thanksgiving

Praise and thanksgiving to you, O Lord our God,
you have given to us the gift of free will, the freedom to choose:
you are a very present help in trouble,
to our weakness you bring your strength.
You are ready to forgive, to renew and to restore us.
You give us the power to grow in grace and to resist evil.
In your strength we can defeat our temptations.
Blessing and praise to you, Father, Son and Holy Spirit.

Intercessions

Lord God, Holy and Strong One,
grant us grace to withstand the temptations of the world, the flesh and all evil. Give to your faithful people the power to stand against wickedness and injustice. May your Church be an instrument of holiness and healing: may it be a bulwark against all that would spoil and mar your creation. Grant, O Lord, that we may respect all that you have made and live to your glory.
Lord, hear us
and deliver us from evil.

Lord God, Holy and Strong One,
give courage and hope to all who suffer through the sin, greed or violence of others. We ask your blessing upon all who are caught up in war, or who are divided against others through ancient or present wrongs. Lord, grant us healing, wholeness and peace.
Lord, hear us
and deliver us from evil.

Lord God, Holy and Strong One,
may your presence and love be revealed to all who have suffered from violence or neglect. We ask your blessing upon all who live where love has grown cold. We remember all who have been betrayed in love and deserted by friends. Lord, guide all who work for reconciliation and peace between peoples.
Lord, hear us
and deliver us from evil.

Lord God, Holy and Strong One,
look with mercy on all who are struggling with life, all who are finding it hard to cope, all who are giving in to despair. We remember before you all who are ill or who are suffering through accidents or acts of violence. May they know your presence and love.
Lord, hear us
and deliver us from evil.

Lord God, Holy and Strong One,
we praise you for your power to defeat evil and darkness, for the forgiveness of sins and the promise of life eternal. Lord, in all our doings, keep us true and faithful to you.
Merciful Father,
accept these prayers for the sake of your Son,
our Saviour Jesus Christ.
Amen.

Collect

Almighty God,
whose Son fasted forty days in the wilderness,
and was tempted as we are, yet without sin:
give us grace to discipline ourselves
in obedience to your Spirit;
and as you know our weakness,
so may we know your power to save;
through Jesus Christ your Son our Lord,
who is alive and reigns with you,
in the unity of the Holy Spirit,
one God, now and for ever.

Common Worship Collect for Lent 1

The Lord's Prayer

Silence

Hymn
Lead us, heavenly Father, lead us

Blessing

The Lord deliver you from all evil:
the Lord strengthen you in all goodness:
the Lord give you grace to grow in holiness:
and the blessing of God Almighty,
the Father, the Son and the Holy Spirit
be upon you and remain with you always.
Amen.

Lent 2
The battle against evil

Affirmation of God's presence

Affirmation

As long as we are alive, we are called to stand against evil and seek to give glory to our God. In the struggle we are not alone. We affirm that our God is ever with us and he is a very present help in trouble.

Invitation to worship

Rejoice, for we live in the presence, the power and the protection of God, Father, Son and Holy Spirit.

The Lord is here.
His Spirit is with us.

Hymn

Stand up, stand up for Jesus

Silence

Litany

God the Father,
have mercy upon us.

God the Son,
have mercy upon us.

God the Holy Spirit,
have mercy upon us.

Holy and blessed Trinity,
have mercy upon us.

Jesus, in our striving for justice,
be with us and help us.

Jesus, in our working for freedom,
be with us and help us.

Jesus, in our seeking peace,
be with us and help us.

Jesus, in our desire to serve you,
be with us and help us.

Jesus, in our longing for your kingdom,
be with us and help us.

Silence

Ministry of the Word

Old Testament
Isaiah 53:1–5

Hymn
All my hope on God is founded

The Gospel
Matthew 12:22–32

Sermon

Silence

Hymn
Soldiers of Christ, arise

Response

Creed

Confession

Thanksgiving

Praise and thanks to you, O Lord, for you are a very present help in all our troubles. You are our shield and protector and strength in our weakness. We rejoice that in the struggle against evil we are never left on our own for you are always with us. We give you thanks that Jesus Christ, your Son our Lord, triumphed over the powers of darkness and death and opened for us the way that leads to eternal life. Blessed are you Father, Son and Holy Spirit.

Intercessions

Holy and Strong God, you know we are set in the midst of many troubles and dangers. Help us to be aware that we are called by your name, that we belong to you, for in you is our hope and our strength. Protect us from all evil and empower us to live to your praise and glory. We remember in your presence all who are persecuted for their faith, all Christians who are mocked and scorned for their stand against greed and evil, all who risk their lives by standing against injustice and tyranny.
Holy and Mighty One, in all our troubles,
hear us and help us.

Holy and Strong God, you know our fears and our weaknesses, give us the strength to reveal your love. We bring before you all who are caught up in violence, war and oppression. We remember all who are belittled through prejudice or protectionism. We ask your blessing upon the world's poor, homeless, refugees and all who seek to relieve their needs.
Holy and Mighty One, in all our troubles,
hear us and help us.

Holy and Strong God, in your love you save and redeem us. We thank you for our homes and all who love us. We bring before you homes where there is violence or neglect, homes where there is tension

and where love has grown cold. We pray for all who feel lonely or unwanted and all who have suffered abuse.
Holy and Mighty One, in all our troubles,
hear us and help us.

Holy and Strong God, you know our frailty and to us you bring your strength. We remember all who are struggling with life, all who feel embattled and overburdened. We ask your blessing upon all who are ill, especially those who can no longer cope on their own. We pray for all who feel defeated in any way. May they all find in you new courage and hope in their troubles.
Holy and Mighty One, in all our troubles,
hear us and help us.

Holy and Strong God, without you darkness and death triumph: with you is light and life eternal. Bless our loved ones departed with the joy of your presence and the fullness of life eternal.
Merciful Father,
accept these prayers for the sake of your Son, Jesus Christ our Lord. Amen.

Collect

Almighty God,
you show to those that are in error the light of your truth,
that they may return to the way of righteousness:
grant to all who are admitted into the fellowship of Christ's religion,
that they may reject those things that are contrary to their profession,
and follow all things that are agreeable to the same;
through Jesus Christ your Son our Lord,
who is alive and reigns with you,
in the unity of the Holy Spirit, one God, now and for ever.

Common Worship Collect for Lent 2

The Lord's Prayer

Silence

Hymn
Through the night of doubt and sorrow

Blessing

The power of the presence of God protect you
and give you strength to withstand the temptations of the world,
the flesh and the devil: and the blessing of God Almighty,
the Father, the Son and the Holy Spirit be upon you
and remain with you always.
Amen.

Lent 3
Suffering

Affirmation of God's presence

Affirmation

There is no doubt that in this world we will face trouble and suffering, for this is a world of sin. But we are not on our own for our God is with us to help us and sustain us. Let us heed the words of Jesus: 'In the world you face persecution. But take courage; I have conquered the world.'

John 16:33

Invitation to worship

Rejoice, for we are in the mighty hands of God,
the Father, the Son and the Holy Spirit.

The Lord is here,
his Spirit is with us.

Hymn

Praise to the holiest

Silence

Litany

God the Father,
have mercy upon us.

God the Son,
have mercy upon us.

God the Holy Spirit,
have mercy upon us.

Holy and blessed Trinity,
have mercy upon us.

Jesus, man of sorrows and acquainted with grief,
be with us and help us.

Jesus, wounded for our transgressions,
be with us and help us.

Jesus, bruised for our iniquities,
be with us and help us.

Jesus, scorned and rejected,
be with us and help us.

Jesus, by whose wounds we are healed,
be with us and help us.

Silence

Ministry of the Word

Old Testament
Isaiah 43:1–3a, 10–12

Hymn
A man there lived in Galilee

The Gospel
Luke 9:18–27

Sermon

Silence

Hymn
Through all the changing scenes of life

Response

Creed

Confession

Thanksgiving

Praise and thanksgiving belong to you, O Lord our God, for in your love you sent your Son to be our Saviour. He became acquainted with grief and shared in our sorrows: he knows our fears and our troubles. We give thanks, for in him and his cross and passion is our salvation: in him are our hope and our joy. Blessed are you Father, Son and Holy
Spirit.

Intercessions

Mighty God, we bring before you the troubles and dangers of peoples and nations, for in you we trust: in you is our strength and salvation. We come as a Church that is divided and often weak in its outreach. Though our faith is weak it is in you, for you are a mighty God. We remember before you all whose faith is challenged, all who are struggling with doubt. We ask your blessing upon the Church in places where it is persecuted or where it is mocked and scorned.
Lord, you are our strength
and our salvation.

Mighty God, empower all who seek to relieve the suffering of our world. We ask your blessing upon all who work in the healing and rebuilding of society. We bring before you all who are broken by war or have suffered from violence. We remember all refugees and homeless people, all who are in want and in weariness.
Lord, you are our strength
and our salvation.

Mighty God, giver of love, reveal your love to us through our homes and our families. Guide us in our dealing with each other that we may grow in love and awareness of you. Lord, be a strength to all who are feeling unloved or unwanted and all who have been betrayed by a loved one. We remember before you homes where people struggle against violence or neglect.
Lord, you are our strength
and our salvation.

Mighty God, you are our health and salvation. We bring before you all suffering peoples. We remember all who are ill and all who need care and attention. We ask your blessing upon all who feel they are no longer able to cope with life and all who are despairing. We ask you to give strength to all who are caring for loved ones who are ill. Lord, give each and every one a sense of your salvation and courage in their troubles.
Lord, you are our strength
and our salvation.

Mighty God, we give thanks for all who have witnessed to your power even to death. We remember all who have kept faith in you and are now departed from us. We ask your blessing upon our loved ones departed from us to where sorrow and suffering are no more. May we share with all the faithful departed in the joys of your eternal kingdom.
Merciful Father,
accept these prayers for the sake of your Son,
our Saviour Jesus Christ.
Amen.

Collect

Almighty God,
whose most dear Son went not up to joy
but first he suffered pain,
and entered not into glory before he was crucified:
mercifully grant that we walking in the way of the cross,
may find in it none other than the way of life and peace;
through Jesus Christ your Son our Lord,
who is alive and reigns with you,
in the unity of the Holy Spirit,
one God, now and for ever.
Common Worship Collect for Lent 3

The Lord's Prayer

Silence

Hymn
I danced in the morning

Blessing

God the Holy and Strong One,
be a present help in all your troubles,
protect you from all that is evil
and bring you to know the joys of his salvation:
and the blessing of God Almighty,
the Father, the Son and the Holy Spirit
be upon you and your loved ones today and for ever.
Amen.

Lent 4
Mothering Sunday

Affirmation of God's presence

Affirmation

God made us because he loves us and he wants us to love him. He wants us to enjoy his love and the love of each other. God seeks to show us his love through our loving parents and the way we love one another. Jesus said, 'By this everyone will know you are my disciples, if you have love for one another.' (John 13:35) For many years this Fourth Sunday of Lent has been kept as Mothering Sunday. Today we give thanks for our mothers, for their love and for the love of God. Our God promises us: 'As a mother comforts her child, so will I comfort you.'

Isaiah 66:13

Invitation to worship

We live in the light and love of the Lord, the Father, the Son and the Holy Spirit.

The Lord is here.
His Spirit is with us.

Hymn

For the beauty of the earth

Silence

Candle-lighting

As they come into church, give every person or family a candle to light as a 'thank you' and as a prayer for their mother. Have a large box filled with sand that can hold the candles in an appropriate place when they are lit. Remember, all people who come in have had or have a mother; let no one be excluded. Give them a printed copy of the hymn that will be sung during the candle-lighting and tell them to use this prayer at home.

Light a large candle from which all will light their candles.

I light this candle to remind us we live in the light and love of God.
God made us out of his love.
Jesus redeemed us by his love.
The Holy Spirit gives us of his love.
I light this candle in the love of God.
Blessed be God for ever.

Invite all to come forward, either as family groups or groups of individuals, to light their candle as a 'thank you' for their homes and especially their mothers. As people return to their seats all that have come with their mother should give her a hug. Once this is done or during it we will sing our opening prayer.

Prayer (to be sung to the tune of Kum ba yah)

Bless our mother, Lord, every day. (x3)
O Lord, bless her now.

Give her love, O Lord, every day. (x3)
O Lord, bless her now.

Give her joy, O Lord, every day. (x3)
O Lord, bless her now.

Keep her safe, O Lord, every day. (x3)
O Lord, bless her now.

If there are lots of candles, different groups of children could sing this throughout the candle-lighting.

Silence

Ministry of the Word

Old Testament

1 Samuel 1:20–28

Hymn
Praise, my soul, the King of heaven

The Gospel
Luke 2:41–52

Sermon

Silence

Hymn
Bind us together, Lord

Response

Creed

Confession

Thanksgiving
God, we thank you that you give life to all living things. We are your children, loved by you, ever under your care and protection and we belong to you. As we thank you for our life, we give you thanks for our home, our parents and our family. Today, we thank you especially for our mother; for her love and her care for us. Blessed are you, Father, Son and Holy Spirit.

Intercessions
Loving God, as we rejoice in the love of our homes, we give you thanks for your great love. May this church show your love to others, and reach out to others with your love. God, strengthen your whole Church that it may be an instrument of your love and peace. May your Church be a means of reconciliation and healing between peoples and nations.
God of love,
hear our prayer.

Loving God, we thank you for the wonderful world that you have given to us, for the light of the sun, the air we breathe and for water. We thank you for all living things, for all that grows and for food. God bless all who work to provide us with what we need. We remember before you all who are without work, and all unable to provide for their families. We remember all hungry and homeless people.
God of love,
hear our prayer.

Loving God, we ask your blessing upon our homes: keep them in your protection and fill them with love. Give strength and joy to our mothers as they love and care for us. We remember before you families where a loved one is ill or causing trouble. We ask for your help for all who are suffering from lack of love or come from homes where there is tension and broken relationships.
God of love,
hear our prayer.

Loving God, it is a joy to know you are with us in our homes. We ask your blessing upon all who feel lonely or neglected. We remember before you those separated from their loved ones through illness or circumstance. God, give strength to all who are in hospital and all who have been taken into care.
God of love,
hear our prayer.

God of love, we thank you for your eternal love and we pray to you for all our loved ones departed. We remember all who have enriched our lives by their goodness and care. We commit our loved ones and all people to your unfailing love.
Merciful Father,
accept these prayers for the sake of your Son,
our Saviour Jesus Christ.
Amen.

Collect

God of compassion, whose Son Jesus Christ, the child of Mary, shared the life of a home in Nazareth, and on the cross, drew the whole human family to himself: strengthen us in our daily living that in joy and in sorrow we may know the power of your presence to bind together and to heal; through Jesus Christ your Son our Lord, who is alive and reigns with you, In the unity of the Holy Spirit, one God, now and for ever.

Common Worship Collect for Mothering Sunday

The Lord's Prayer

Silence

Hymn

Now thank we all our God

Blessing

The God of life and love,
be with you and your loved ones,
God bless your homes with his presence
and your lives with his peace, God be with you always:
and the blessing of God Almighty,
the Father, the Son and the Holy Spirit,
be upon you and your home now and always.
Amen.

Lent 5
Passion

Affirmation of God's presence

Affirmation

We come before our God who, in his great love, sent his Son to be our Saviour. As we move closer to the events of Good Friday we turn to see the love our Lord has revealed in his passion and his dying for us. Invitation to worship. We are in the love and light of the Lord, the Father, the Son and the Holy Spirit. **Amen.**

The Lord is here.
His Spirit is with us.

Hymn

It is a thing most wonderful

Silence

Litany

God the Father,
have mercy upon us.

God the Son,
have mercy upon us.

God the Holy Spirit,
have mercy upon us.

Holy and blessed Trinity,
have mercy upon us.

By your most glorious passion,
Saviour, strengthen us.

By your suffering on the cross,
Saviour, strengthen us.

By your sacred wounds,
Saviour, strengthen us.

By your hunger and thirst,
Saviour, strengthen us.

By your death and burial,
Saviour, strengthen us.

By your triumph over the grave,
Saviour, strengthen us.

By your glorious resurrection,
Saviour, strengthen us.

Silence

Ministry of the Word

Old Testament
Isaiah 53:1–9

Hymn
Glory be to Jesus

The Gospel
John 12:20–36

Sermon

Silence

Hymn
Take up thy cross, the Saviour said

Response

Creed

Confession

Thanksgiving

Praise and thanks to you, O Lord our God, for you love us with an everlasting love: out of your love you sent your Son, Christ our Lord, to be our Saviour. We give you thanks, O Christ, for by your loving obedience, by your accepting suffering and the cross, yet still giving yourself in love, you have redeemed us. Praise to you, O Christ, by your death and burial you have delivered us from the power of the enemy and opened to us the way to life eternal. Blessing and praise to you, Father, Son and Holy Spirit, one God for ever and ever. **Amen.**

Intercessions

God, our Maker and Redeemer,
we bring before you all who are being persecuted for their faith. We remember all who face mockery and rejection, and all whose lives and homes are endangered. May your holy people triumph over evil and grow in grace. May we witness to you and your saving power.
By your cross and passion,
save us and help us, O Lord.

God, our Maker and Redeemer,
we bring before you peoples and nations that are divided through hatred and war. We remember all who have lost homes and loved ones, all who are caught up in violence. We ask your blessing upon all refugees, all who are without work and those who have lost hope or confidence in you.
By your cross and passion,
save us and help us, O Lord.

God, our Maker and Redeemer,
we bring before you our homes and loved ones. Bless our families and friends. May we live in good fellowship with all our neighbours. We remember before you homes where there is a lack of love, where there is division and where there is much sorrow.
By your cross and passion,
save us and help us, O Lord.

God, our Maker and Redeemer,
we bring before you all suffering people, all who cry out in loneliness and pain. We remember especially any who have suffered from acts of violence, all who have been injured in accidents and all whose lives are endangered. We ask your blessing on all who are giving their life in the service and love of others.
By your cross and passion,
save us and help us, O Lord.

God, our Maker and Redeemer,
we bring before you all who are facing death today, expected or unexpected. We remember our loved ones who are departed from us and we ask your blessing on all who have died in the faith of Christ. We commend all to your mercy and protection.
Merciful Father,
accept these prayers for the sake of your Son,
our Saviour Jesus Christ.
Amen.

Collect

Most merciful God,
who by the death and resurrection of your Son Jesus Christ delivered and saved the world:
grant that by faith in him who suffered on the cross we may triumph in the power of his victory;
through Jesus Christ your Son our Lord,
who is alive and reigns with you,
in the unity of the Holy Spirit,
one God, now and for ever.

Common Worship Collect for Lent 5

The Lord's Prayer

Silence

Hymn
When I survey the wondrous cross

Blessing

The love of Christ give you hope,
the offering of Christ strengthen you in his service,
the cross of Christ deliver you from all evil,
the death of Christ open to you the way to life eternal:
and the blessing of God Almighty,
the Father, the Son, and the Holy Spirit
be upon you and remain with you always.
Amen.

Palm Sunday

Affirmation of God's presence

Affirmation

Today we share in the joys and sorrows of our Lord. We remember his joyful entry into Jerusalem with the waving of palms. But our palms are in the shape of a cross for we move through the events of Holy Week to the Passion and the crucifixion of our Lord.
Palm crosses are given out either as people enter the church or at this point.

Invitation to worship

We are in the presence of God the Father our Creator, of Christ the King our Redeemer, of the Holy Spirit who empowers us.

The Lord is here.
His Spirit is with us.

Blessing of the Palms

Ask the people to hold up their crosses as this prayer is said.
God our Father, whose Son our Saviour entered Jerusalem as the Christ to suffer and to die for us all, bless these palm crosses. May they remind us of all that Christ has done for us. May we welcome him into our lives and homes. Grant that we who welcome him as King follow in his way until we come to the fullness of life eternal. We ask this in the name of him who is our King and Saviour, Jesus Christ our Lord.

Hosanna to the Son of David.
Blessed is he who comes in the name of the Lord.
Hosanna in the highest.

The Gospel

Year A Matthew 21:1–11
Year B Mark 11:1–11
Year C Luke 19:28–40

Hymn

All glory, laud and honour *(if possible there should be a procession of all who are holding the palm crosses during this hymn.)*

Prayer

Lord Jesus,
as you were welcomed when you entered into Jerusalem
with palms and shouts of praise,
we rejoice in your coming to us this day
and pray that you may enter into our lives
and the life of our community
as our Lord and King;
to you be all glory and honour,
who lives and reigns with the Father
and the Holy Spirit,
One God, now and for ever.

Silence

Ministry of the Word

Old Testament

Isaiah 53:4–9

Hymn

Ride on, ride on in majesty

Gospel readings from the Passion of our Lord and Saviour

After each reading, sing a hymn, verse of a hymn or keep silence.

Jesus is betrayed
Year A Matthew 26:30–56
Year B Mark 14:32–50
Year C Luke 22:39–53

Hymn

It is a thing most wonderful

Jesus is denied
Year A Matthew 26:69–75
Year B Mark 14:53–54, 66–72
Year C Luke 22:54–61

Hymn
My God I love thee

Jesus is condemned
Year A Matthew 27:1, 2, 11–26
Year B Mark 15:1–15
Year C Luke 23:1–4, 13–25

Hymn
O my Saviour lifted

Jesus is crucified
Year A Matthew 27:32–50, 54
Year B Mark 15:22–39
Year C Luke 23:26, 32–47

Silence

Hymn
Glory be to Jesus

Response

Creed

Confession

Thanksgiving
Thanks be to you, my Lord Jesus Christ,
for all the benefits you have won for me,
for all the pains and insults you have borne for me.
O most merciful Redeemer, Friend and Brother,
may I know you more clearly,
love you more dearly,

and follow you more nearly,
day by day.
St Richard of Chichester 1197–1253

Intercessions

Praise to you, King of eternal glory,
we rejoice with all who welcome you into their hearts and homes.
Bless your Church, may it be an instrument of peace, and in praising you lead others to know you.
We remember all who preach and teach in your name, and all who are seeking to follow you faithfully.
Jesus, Lamb of God,
hear us and help us.

Praise to you, King of eternal glory,
we rejoice with all who are aware of you in the midst of the city,
in the midst of commerce and trade. Bless all who witness to you through fair dealing and justice, through striving for freedom and in the caring for others. We remember before you Jerusalem and all its troubles, and long for peace in our world.
Jesus, Lamb of God,
hear us and help us.

Praise to you, King of eternal glory,
we rejoice with all who reveal your presence through love.
Bless our families and friends and all our community. We remember all who feel that they do not belong anywhere, especially any who are scorned, persecuted and rejected.
Jesus, Lamb of God,
hear us and help us.

Praise to you, King of eternal glory,
we rejoice with all who proclaim you as their Lord and Saviour.
Bless all who give their lives in the service of others, especially those who seek to relieve pain and suffering. We remember those who are ill and who have sorrow, especially any who are despairing and losing faith.
Jesus, Lamb of God,
hear us and help us.

Praise to you, King of eternal glory,
we rejoice with all who have remained faithful to you even to death. Bless our loved ones departed, that they may know you as their God and Saviour. We remember all who have died this day and all who mourn: may we all know that in you, and you alone, is life eternal.
Merciful Father,
accept these prayers for the sake of our Saviour, Jesus Christ.
Amen.

Collect
Almighty Father,
look with mercy on this your family
for which our Lord Jesus Christ
was content to be betrayed
and given up into the hand of sinners
and to suffer death upon the cross;
who is alive and glorified
with you and the Holy Spirit, one God, now and for ever.

Common Worship Collect for Good Friday

The Lord's Prayer

Silence

Hymn
There is a green hill

Blessing

The cross of Christ
defend you from all evil,
strengthen you in your love for him,
keep you firm in the faith,
give you comfort in your sorrows,
and rescue you from death:
and the blessing of God Almighty,
the Father, the Son and the Holy Spirit
be upon you and your loved ones, now and ever more.
Amen.

Good Friday
The Way of The Cross

How to pray the Stations

The Way of the Cross, often called the Stations of the Cross, is found in the Catholic, Anglican and Lutheran traditions. It may be used at any time of the year but especially on Fridays in Lent and on Good Friday. It makes a good personal devotion and can be used for meditation using just one or two stations a day or spending time to travel to all of the stations.

The Stations of the Cross began in Jerusalem on the Via Dolorosa (the Sorrowful Way) where pilgrims sought to stop, pray and meditate at various places where tradition said certain events happened. Some of the stations had no basis in Scripture, though they could well have happened, and were used to illustrate the fullness of the saving acts. The non-Scriptural stations are the three falls of Jesus, Jesus meeting his mother, and Veronica wiping his face. The stations were found in artwork or carvings all over Europe by the fifteenth century. Possibly the devotion arose especially for pilgrims who could not hope to travel to Jerusalem. The Stations of the Cross have provided a visual devotion for countless Christians. The number of stations has varied – some would restrict them to the biblically based stations – but usually there are now the fourteen stations.

Above all, it must be remembered that the stations are an act of pilgrimage: this is not an intellectual exercise but an act of devotion. The heart and the imagination have to be able to come into play. The stations are a journey in awareness not only of historical events but also of 'the lamb that was slain before the foundation of the world' (Revelation 13:8); awareness of the presence of the Lord in our lives, in our suffering and in suffering humanity. The Way of the Cross travels through our world and is present wherever someone is betrayed by a kiss or deserted by loved ones; wherever anyone suffers injustice or enters into darkness. Christ is found with the poor and the powerless, with the scorned and rejected. In the midst of all life the Lord is there. The Way of the Cross is a journey with our Lord. It is a journey into the love of God as revealed in his Son

Jesus Christ. The crucified one knows our troubles and he is with us always.

We are faced with wonder and mystery. God comes down: the Creator is in the hands of his creation. The Maker of the world is edged out of the world, out of the city, out of lives and on to the cross. He who came to set us free is fixed by nails; he who came to give life is put to death. What is the meaning of all of this? We are to learn that love is his meaning. He comes to us out of love, gives himself in love and love holds him on the cross. The best preparation for us to enter into this wonder and mystery is silence and stillness. We stand before events that the mind can hardly grasp, but the heart can feel. Do not rush the stations; take your time with each one and enter into stillness – stations are where you stop for a while. Pause in the presence and let the power and love of God enfold you, and give your love to him.

Begin the stations with a personal prayer that centres on the presence and love of God. Be still and quiet and give your love to him.

In the saving power of God, Father,
Son and Holy Spirit.

Blessed are you Lord God of our salvation,
in your love for us
you gave us your Son to be our Redeemer.
As we walk the way of the cross,
may we walk with Christ our Lord
and know his great love for us.
As he gave himself for us,
help us to give our life to you,
blessed Father, Son and Holy Spirit.

First station
Jesus is condemned to death

We adore you, O Christ, and we bless you,
because by your holy cross you have redeemed the world.

He was despised and rejected by others; a man of suffering and acquainted with infirmity . . . Surely he has borne our infirmities and carried our diseases . . . He was wounded for our transgressions, crushed for our iniquities; upon him was the punishment that made us whole, and by his bruises we are healed. All we like sheep have gone astray; we have all turned to our own way, and the Lord has laid on him the iniquity of us all. He was oppressed, and he was afflicted, yet he did not open his mouth; like a lamb that is led to the slaughter, and like a sheep that before its shearers is silent, so he did not open his mouth.

Isaiah 53:3-7

The powers of this world are determined to be rid of Jesus.
He challenges their way of life,
their power structures,
their luxury whilst others starve,
their insensitivity towards their fellows,
and for this he is condemned.

The church people are not comfortable with him.
He talks about their dedication.
He questions their lack of mission.
He wants them to love as God loves,
and for this he is condemned.

He came in love and they vent their hatred upon him.
He came to enrich their lives and they strip him and leave him bare.
He came to give life and they condemn him to death.
He sought to set them free and they fix him to a cross of wood.

Jesus, help us to accept you as our Lord and our God.
Increase our sensitivity to your presence in others:
help us to know that as we do it to the least of all we do it to you.

Lord Jesus Christ, who by your cross and passion
have redeemed us,
save and help us, we humbly beseech you, O Lord.

Second station
Jesus receives the cross

We adore you, O Christ, and we bless you,
because by your holy cross you have redeemed the world.

'The Son of Man must undergo great suffering, and be rejected by the elders, chief priests and scribes, and be killed, and on the third day be raised.' Then he said to them all, 'If any want to become my followers, let them deny themselves and take up their cross daily and follow me. For those who want to save their life will lose it, and those who lose their life for my sake will save it. What does it profit them if they gain the whole world, but lose or forfeit themselves?'

Here is the cross.
Take it as if it is yours, as if you deserved it.
Take upon you the injustice, the cruelty
and the hatred of the world.
Take upon you all the pain and sorrow.
Lord, you give yourself in love –
let me not give a cross to you.

Jesus, we remember all who are forced to accept
suffering as their daily lot,
all who are betrayed by loved ones,
all deserted by their friends,
all who are very much left alone.
In you may they find hope.

Lord Jesus Christ, who by your cross and passion
have redeemed us,
save and help us, we humbly beseech you, O Lord.

Third station
Jesus falls for the first time

We adore you, O Christ, and we bless you,
because by your holy cross you have redeemed the world.

Cursed is the ground because of you; in toil you shall eat of it all the days of your life; thorns and thistles it shall bring forth for you; and you shall eat the plants of the field. By the sweat of your face you shall eat bread until you return to the ground, for out of it you were taken; you are dust, and to dust you shall return.

Genesis 3:17-19

The Son of Man is weakened;
a heart is breaking with love.
He came down to lift us up,
and now he descends to the dust.
God and dust mix together.
He humbled himself unto death,
even death on the cross.
Now he crawls in the dust – see how the dust clings
to him as he arises!
He comes down to the lowest level to raise us up.

Lord Jesus, many are your humiliations:
born in a stable, taken as a refugee,
scorned and rejected, betrayed with a kiss,
denied by a friend, deserted by disciples,
brought down to the dust.
We remember before you
all who suffer humiliation and all who are brought low.

Lord Jesus Christ, who by your cross and passion
have redeemed us,
save and help us, we humbly beseech you, O Lord.

Fourth station
Jesus is met by his mother

We adore you, O Christ, and we bless you,
because by your holy cross you have redeemed the world.

Then Simeon blessed them and said to his mother Mary, 'This child is destined for the falling and the rising of many in Israel, and to be a sign that will be opposed so that the inner thoughts of many will be revealed – and a sword will pierce your own soul too.'

Luke 2:34, 35

Mary ought not to have come, but love drew her to him.
This would cost her much pain and sorrow, agony
  and awful memories.
Why should this happen to him, to her?
What had either done to deserve this?
There seemed to be no answer.

Pain is not a private thing; it is shared by loved ones.
If one suffers, all suffer.
Mary experiences the sword that was to pierce her heart.

Lord, we fear that if we love you,
we will be asked to walk the way of the cross.
If we give you our hearts,
it will be pierced with the sorrows of the world.

Lord Jesus Christ, who by your cross and passion
have redeemed us,
save and help us, we humbly beseech you, O Lord.

Fifth station
Simon of Cyrene is compelled to carry the cross

We adore you, O Christ, and we bless you,
because by your holy cross you have redeemed the world.

They compelled a passer-by, who was coming in from the country, to carry his cross; it was Simon of Cyrene, the father of Alexander and Rufus. Then they brought Jesus to the place called Golgotha (which means the place of a skull).

Mark 15:21, 22

Simon is an African, as Cyrene was what is now Libya.
He had no intentions of doing anything.
He was entering the city from the country.
He is forced to carry the cross.
That day he learnt something that would change him –
for we are told his sons are known by the Church.
Military rule forces its will on people.
People are still compelled to do awful things.
The cross is to be borne in our helping of the least,
in the hungry,
the refugee,
the homeless,
the outcasts.
The Lord calls us to bear one another's burdens.

Lord, as you have given your life for us,
help us to give ourselves to others
and to you.

Lord Jesus Christ, who by your cross and passion
have redeemed us,
save and help us, we humbly beseech you, O Lord.

Sixth station
Veronica wipes the face of Jesus

We adore you, O Christ, and we bless you,
because by your holy cross you have redeemed the world.

Hear, O Lord, when I cry aloud,
be gracious to me and answer me!
'Come,' my heart says, 'seek his face!'
Your face, Lord, do I seek.
Do not hide your face from me.
Psalm 27:7-9

Jesus had been badly beaten.
His face is covered with sweat, dust and blood.
He is not a pretty sight.
One in the crowd is moved by his suffering.
She comes forward and stands out from the crowd.
She disregards the danger and the hostility;
she acts on impulse out of love.
It is said that the face of Jesus was captured on the cloth she used to wipe his face.
She would keep this image in her heart.
She would remember this face, a face like any other face,
but she had looked into the eyes of God.
The face of God is scarred by thorns,
bloodied by violence.

Lord, how often we defile your image
and mar your likeness.
Forgive us and help us to reveal you to others.

Lord Jesus Christ, who by your cross and passion
have redeemed us,
save and help us, we humbly beseech you, O Lord.

Seventh station
Jesus falls for a second time

We adore you, O Christ, and we bless you,
because by your holy cross you have redeemed the world.

My soul clings to the dust;
revive me according to your word.
My soul melts away for sorrow;
strengthen me according to your word.
Let your steadfast love come to me, O Lord,
your salvation according to your promise.
Then shall I have an answer for those who taunt me,
for I trust in your word.

Psalm 119:25, 28, 41, 42

Lord, do you never give up?
You are down again –
and we know it will not be for the last time.
How long must you suffer?
How long can your creation defile and degrade you?
Once again you bite the dust for us
and for our salvation.
Dust and divinity mingling together:
dust rising with you when you arise.

Lord, when we attach myself to you, we arise,
for with you is life and life eternal.

Lord Jesus Christ, who by your cross and passion
have redeemed us,
save and help us, we humbly beseech you, O Lord.

Eighth station
Jesus meets the women of Jerusalem

We adore you, O Christ, and we bless you,
because by your holy cross you have redeemed the world.

A great number of people followed him, and among them were women who were beating their breasts and wailing for him. But Jesus turned to them and said, 'Daughters of Jerusalem, do not weep for me, but weep for yourselves and for your children. For the days are surely coming when they will say, "Blessed are the barren, and the wombs that never bore, and the breasts that never nursed." Then they will begin to say to the mountains, "Fall on us"; and to the hills, "Cover us." For if they do this when the wood is green, what will happen when it is dry?'

Luke 23:27-31

Only the hardened and the toughest of people would
  not be moved,
but many regimes brutalise people.
Some women are openly weeping for Jesus;
  their hearts are stirred.
The mothers know a mother's heart must be breaking.
It causes tears to flow.
The sorrow of women for their children
  is a great sorrow.
Jesus accepts their sympathy – but with a warning.
More than tears are needed to change the world.
If they can do this to a just man,
what will they do to others?
If this can be done to the Son of God,
then no one is safe.

Lord, we come to you in sorrow
for the suffering peoples of the world.
Give us the courage and willpower to help where we can.

Lord Jesus Christ, who by your cross and passion
have redeemed us,
save and help us, we humbly beseech you, O Lord.

Ninth station
Jesus falls for the third time

We adore you, O Christ, and we bless you,
because by your holy cross you have redeemed the world.

Christ Jesus who, though he was in the form of God,
did not regard equality with God
as something to be exploited,
but emptied himself,
taking the form of a slave,
being born in human likeness.
And being found in human form,
he humbled himself
and became obedient to the point of death –
even death on a cross.

Philippians 2:6-8

There you go, down again. This is becoming a habit.
You seem to be attached to the dust.
This time it looks as if this is it: are you still breathing?
Shall we count you out? We could count you out.
Are you already dead?
How long do you want to lie there: three days or more?
Death is not far away – but you rise again.

Lord Jesus, as the dust clings to you as you rise,
may we hold fast to you and to your saving power.

Lord Jesus Christ, who by your cross and passion
have redeemed us,
save and help us, we humbly beseech you, O Lord.

Tenth station
Jesus is stripped of his garments

We adore you, O Christ, and we bless you,
because by your holy cross you have redeemed the world.

My God, my God, why have you forsaken me?
Why are you so far from helping me,
from the words of my groaning?
I am poured out like water,
and all my bones are out of joint;
my heart is like wax;
it is melted within my breast;
my mouth is dried up like a potsherd,
and my tongue sticks to my jaws;
you lay me in the dust of death.
For dogs are all around me;
a company of evildoers encircles me.
My hands and feet have shrivelled;
I can count all my bones.
They stare and gloat over me;
they divide my clothes among themselves,
and for my clothing they cast lots.
But you, O Lord, do not be far away!
O my help, come quickly to my aid!
Psalm 22:1, 14-18

They have taken all from you.
Now they gamble for the robe your mother gave you.
They take away your dignity and leave you exposed.
They strip you of your humanity
and will take away your life.
There is no Transfiguration, no white robes,
only bareness;
nothing to shield you from the cross or from mockery.
You are defenceless or so it seems.
Yet in love you allow all this for us.
Lord, strip from us all false pride;
strip away all self-trust;
take away all that keeps us from you.

We remember before you all who are laid bare,
all who have nothing and are counted as nothing.

Lord Jesus Christ, who by your cross and passion
have redeemed us,
save and help us, we humbly beseech you, O Lord.

Eleventh station
Jesus is nailed to the cross

We adore you, O Christ, and we bless you,
because by your holy cross you have redeemed the world.

So they took Jesus; and carrying the cross by himself, he went out to what is called The Place of the Skull, which in Hebrew is called Golgotha. There they crucified him, and with him two others, one on either side, with Jesus between them. Pilate also had an inscription written and put on the cross. It read, 'Jesus of Nazareth, the King of the Jews.' Many of the Jews read this inscription, because the place where Jesus was crucified was near the city; and it was written in Hebrew, in Latin and in Greek.

John 19:16b-20

Jesus who came to set them free is fixed . . .
to a cross of wood.
Listen to the sound of the nails.
Iron on iron, iron into wood, all resound.
Human flesh does not make much sound,
neither does the Son of Man.
Here is planned cruelty and indignity.
Jesus is hung like a picture – but not a pretty sight.
Arms are stretched out as if to welcome in an embrace.
This is the cost of your love, of the love of God.
The Christ is poured out for us and for our salvation.

Lord, as you open your arms to welcome us,
let us remember the cost.
By your agony and loneliness,
support us in my troubles.
By your life laid down,
lift us up and bring us to life eternal.

Lord Jesus Christ, who by your cross and passion
have redeemed us,
save and help us, we humbly beseech you, O Lord.

Twelfth station
Jesus dies upon the cross

We adore you, O Christ, and we bless you,
because by your holy cross you have redeemed the world.

When it was noon, darkness came over the whole land until three in the afternoon. At three o'clock Jesus cried out with a loud voice, 'Eloi, Eloi, lema sabachthani?' which means, 'My God, my God, why have you forsaken me?' When some of the bystanders heard it, they said, 'Listen, he is calling for Elijah.' And someone ran, filled a sponge with sour wine, put it on a stick, and gave it to him to drink, saying, 'Wait, let us see whether Elijah will come to take him down.' Then Jesus gave a loud cry and breathed his last.

Mark 15:33-37

Can it be that God suffers for us?
Can it be that God dies for us?
The Christ has paid the extreme price of love:
he has laid down his life for us;
through him the darkness is banished.
He has served his Father faithfully even to death,
and in death he has become our Redeemer.
There is no greater love than this.

Lord Christ, our Redeemer,
as you give yourself for us and to us,
help us to give ourselves to you.

Lord Jesus Christ, who by your cross and passion
have redeemed us,
save and help us, we humbly beseech you, O Lord.

Thirteenth station
Jesus is taken down from the cross

We adore you, O Christ, and we bless you,
because by your holy cross you have redeemed the world.

When his parents saw him they were astonished; and his mother said to him, 'Child, why have you treated us like this? Look, your father and I have been searching for you in great anxiety.' He said to them, 'Why were you searching for me? Did you not know that I must be in my Father's house?'

Luke 2:48, 49

Once again Jesus returns to his mother's lap.
But there is no joy here: the body is broken
  and disfigured.
A sword pierces her own heart.
How long is it since he was last in her arms?
This is a far cry from Bethlehem and Nazareth:
there was so much promise;
it seemed the whole world would follow him.
Now Jesus, her son, is dead.
He came to his own but his own received him not.
The creature has sought to kill the Creator.
What hells are let loose on the world?

Lord Christ,
We remember all who are facing death
or the death of a loved one.
We pray for all who have been killed
through violence or accidents.
Lord, in your death may we find hope.

Lord Jesus Christ, who by your cross and passion
have redeemed us,
save and help us, we humbly beseech you, O Lord.

Fourteenth station
Jesus is laid in the tomb

We adore you, O Christ, and we bless you,
because by your holy cross you have redeemed the world.

When evening had come, and since it was the day of Preparation, that is, the day before the Sabbath, Joseph of Arimathea, a respected member of the council, who was also himself waiting expectantly for the kingdom of God, went boldly to Pilate and asked for the body of Jesus. Then Pilate wondered if he were already dead; and summoning the centurion, he asked him whether he had been dead for some time. When he learned from the centurion that he was dead, he granted the body to Joseph. Then Joseph bought a linen cloth, and taking down the body, wrapped it in the linen cloth, and laid it in a tomb that had been hewn out of the rock. He then rolled a stone against the door of the tomb. Mary Magdalene and Mary the mother of Joses saw where the body was laid.

Mark 15:42-47

As the sun goes down, the Christ is buried
in a borrowed grave.
After all the pain and agony he looks at rest:
the whiteness of the linen cloth
helps to hide the wounds and scars.
He lies here like a seed buried in the earth.
This is the winter of the world:
all who love him are left numbed and cold,
exhausted and empty.
At least he has passed beyond it all.

Lord Jesus, come into our darkness,
into our lives sealed against feeling,
into our many deaths.
Help us to know that you are beyond the grave
and beckon us to glory.

Lord Jesus Christ, who by your cross and passion
have redeemed us,
save and help us, we humbly beseech you, O Lord.

Easter

Easter Vigil

This holy night, we come before great mysteries.
He, who made the earth, is buried within it.
He, who gives life to all things, lies in the grave.
He, who comes to set us free, is held by the tomb.
He, who gives light to the world, has entered into darkness.
He, who created the heavens, has descended into hell.
All creation waits in expectation and longs for the redemption he brings.

This holy night, we gather in vigil and prayer,
for this is the Passover of our Lord.
He is the Lamb of God that takes away the sins of the world.
This holy night, the Lord of love is victorious over all hatred.
This holy night, the Lord of light conquers the darkness.
This holy night, the Lord of life triumphs over death.

This holy night, as we await the risen Christ,
we hear again of God's saving acts in history.
We recall how he redeemed his people in the past
and in the fullness of time sent his Son to be our Redeemer.
Let us pray that through our Easter celebration,
we may know in our lives the presence and power of the risen Lord.

Silence

Light out of darkness *Genesis 1:1–5a, 26, 27*

Narrator In the beginning when God created the universe, the earth was a formless void, and darkness covered the face of the deep, while a wind from God swept over the face of the waters. Then God said,

God Let there be light.

Narrator And there was light. And God saw that the light was good; and God separated the light from the darkness. God called the light

God Day!

Narrator And the darkness he called

God Night!

Pause

Narrator Then God said,

God Let us make humankind in our own image, according to our likeness; and let them have dominion over the fish of the sea, and over all the birds of the air, and over the cattle, and over all the wild animals of earth, and over every creeping thing that creeps on the earth.

Narrator So God created humankind in his image, in the image of God he created them; male and female he created them.

Reader Our God is the God of all, the God of heaven and earth, the God of the sea, of rivers, of sun and moon and stars, of the lofty mountains and the lowly valleys.
The God above heaven.
The God under heaven.
The God in heaven.
He has his dwelling around heaven,
and earth and sea, and all that is in them.
He quickens all.
He dominates all.
He inspires all.

St Patrick

Collect

Almighty God,
who wonderfully created us in your own image
and yet more wonderfully restored us,
through your Son Jesus Christ;
grant that as he came to share our humanity,
so may we share in his divinity;
who is alive and reigns with you and the Holy Spirit,
One God now and for ever.

Music

Be still and know that I am God

Into the dark *Genesis 3:8–11, 17–19, 23, 24*

Narrator The first story of mankind tells us how Adam and Eve disobeyed God by eating of the fruit of the forbidden tree and were turned out of the garden. By disobedience we turn our back on God and his bounty.

They heard the sound of the Lord God walking in the garden at the time of the evening breeze, and the man and his wife hid themselves from the presence of the Lord God among the trees of the garden. But the Lord called to the man and said to him,

God Where are you?

Adam I heard the sound of you in the garden and I was afraid, because I was naked; and I hid myself.

God Who told you that you were naked? Have you eaten from the tree which I commanded you not to eat?

Adam The woman whom you gave to be with me, she gave me of the fruit of the tree, and I ate.

God Because you have listened to the voice of your wife and have eaten of the tree which I commanded you, 'You shall not eat of it,' cursed is the ground because of you; in toil you shall eat of it all the days of your life; thorns and thistles it shall bring forth for you; and you shall eat the plants of the field. By the sweat of your face you shall eat bread until you return to the ground, for out of it you were taken; you are dust and to dust you shall return.

Narrator Therefore the Lord sent him forth from the garden of Eden, to till the ground from which he was taken. He drove out the man; and at the east of the garden of Eden he placed the cherubim, and a sword flaming and turning to guard the way to the tree of life.

Collect

Heavenly Father,
whose blessed Son was revealed to destroy the works of the devil,
and to make us children of God and heirs of eternal life:
grant that we, having this hope, may purify ourselves,
even as he is pure: that when he shall appear in power
and great glory we may be made like him,
in his eternal and glorious kingdom:
where he is alive and reigns with you
and the Holy Spirit, One God, now and for ever.
Amen.

Common Worship, Times and Seasons p.377

At this point put out all the lights in the building except a small light at the lectern. Better still if readers could use a small torch.

Music

O Lord, hear our prayer

Rescue from chaos

Genesis 6:5, 6, 13, 14, 18, 19, 22; 7:4, 17, 18, 24; 8:1, 6–13, 18; 9:8–13

Narrator The Lord saw the wickedness of humankind was great in the earth, and every inclination of the thoughts of their hearts was only evil continually. And the Lord was sorry that he had made humankind on the earth, and it grieved him to his heart . . . and God said to Noah, **God** I have determined to make an end of all flesh; for the earth is filled with violence because of them; now I am going to destroy them along with the earth. Make yourself an ark of cypress wood; make rooms in the ark and cover it inside and out with pitch . . . I will establish my covenant with you; and you shall come into the ark, you, your sons, your wife and your sons' wives with you. And of every living thing, of all flesh, you shall bring two of every kind into the ark, to keep them alive with you; they shall be male and female . . . In seven days I will send rain on the earth for forty days and forty nights.

Narrator Noah did this; he did all that God commanded him . . . The flood continued for forty days on the earth; and the waters increased and bore up the ark and it rose high above the earth. The waters swelled and increased greatly on the earth; and the ark floated on the face of the waters . . . and the waters swelled for one hundred and fifty days.

But God remembered Noah and all the wild animals and all the domestic animals that were with him in the ark. And God made a wind blow over the earth, and the waters subsided . . . At the end of forty days, Noah opened the window of the ark he had made and sent out the raven; and it went to and fro until the waters were dried up from the earth. Then he sent out the dove from him, to see if the waters had subsided from the face of the ground; but the dove found no place to set its foot, and it returned to him to the ark for the waters were still on the face of the whole earth. He waited another seven days and again sent out the dove from the ark, and the dove came back to him in the evening and there in its beak was a freshly plucked olive leaf. Noah knew that the waters had subsided from the earth. Then he waited another seven days, and sent out the dove: it did not return to him any more . . . So Noah went out with his sons and his wife, and his sons' wives. God said to Noah and to his sons with him,

God I am establishing my covenant with you and with your descendants, and with every living creature that is with you . . . that never again shall all flesh be cut off by the waters of a flood . . . This is the sign of the covenant that I make between me and you and every living creature that is with you, for all future generations: I have set my bow in the clouds, and it shall be a sign of the covenant between me and the earth.

Prayer

Lord, from this world's stormy sea,
give your hand for lifting me.
Lift me up from darkest night.

Lift me to the realms of light.
Lord, lift me up from body's pain.
Lift me up and keep me sane.
Lord, lift me from the things I dread.
Lift me from the living dead.
Lord, lift me from the place I lie.
Lift me that I never die.

Music
Do not be afraid

God will provide a sacrifice *Genesis 22:1–18*

Narrator God tested Abraham. He said to him, **God** Abraham!

Abraham Here I am, Lord.

God Take your son, your only son, Isaac, whom you love, and go to the land of Moriah and offer him there as a burnt offering on one of the mountains that I shall show you.

Narrator So Abraham rose early in the morning, saddled his donkey, and took two of his young men with him, and his son Isaac; he cut the wood for the burnt offering, and set out and went to the place in the distance that God had shown him. On the third day Abraham looked and saw the place far away. Then Abraham said to his young men,

Abraham Stay here with the donkey; the boy and I will go over there; we will worship, and then we will come back to you.

Narrator Abraham took the wood for the burnt offering, and laid it on his son Isaac: and he himself took the fire and the knife. So the two of them walked on together. Isaac said to his father Abraham,

Isaac Father!

Abraham Here I am, my son.

Isaac The fire and the wood are here, but where is the lamb for a burnt offering?

Abraham God himself will provide the lamb for a burnt offering, my son.

Narrator So the two of them walked on together. When they came to the place that God had shown him, Abraham built an altar there, and laid the wood in order. He bound his son Isaac, and laid him on the altar, on top of the wood. Then Abraham reached out his hand, and took the knife to kill his son. But the angel of the Lord called to him from heaven,

God Abraham, Abraham!

Abraham Here I am.

God Do not lay your hand on the boy or do anything to harm him; for now I know that you fear God, since you have not withheld your son, your only son, from me.

Narrator Abraham looked up and saw a ram, caught in a thicket by his horns. Abraham went and took the ram and offered it up as a burnt offering instead of his son. So Abraham called that place 'The Lord will provide' . . . The angel of the Lord called Abraham a second time from heaven and said,

God By myself I have sworn, because you have done this and have not withheld your son, your only son, I will indeed bless you. I will make your offspring as numerous as the stars of heaven and as the sand that is on the seashore. By your offspring shall all the nations of the earth gain blessings for themselves, because you have obeyed my voice.

Collect

Almighty God, whose chosen servant Abraham
faithfully obeyed your call and rejoiced in your promises,
that, in him, all the families of the earth should be blessed,
give us faith like his, that in us your promises may be fulfilled,
through Jesus Christ our Lord.

Common Worship, Times and Seasons p.379

Music

Praise God from whom all blessings flow

He will save us from our foes *Exodus 14:5, 6 10, 11, 13–16, 21–30*

Narrator When the king of Egypt was told that the people of Israel had fled . . . he had his chariot made ready and took his army with him . . . As Pharaoh drew near, the Israelites looked back, and there were the Egyptians advancing on them. In great fear the Israelites cried out to the Lord. They said to Moses,

Chorus Was it because there were no graves in Egypt that you have taken us away to die in the wilderness?

Narrator But Moses said to the people,

Moses Do not be afraid, stand firm and see the deliverance that the Lord will accomplish for you today; for the Egyptians whom you see today you shall never see again. The Lord will fight for you, and you only have to keep still.

Narrator Then the Lord said to Moses,

God Why do you cry out to me? Tell the Israelites to go forward. But you lift up your staff and stretch out your hand over the sea and divide it, that the Israelites may go into the sea on dry ground.

Narrator Then Moses stretched out his hand over the sea. The Lord drove the sea back by a strong east wind all night, and turned the sea into dry land; and the waters were divided. The Israelites went into the sea on dry ground, the waters forming a wall for them on their right and on their left. The Egyptians pursued, and went in after them into the midst of the sea, all of Pharaoh's horses, chariots and his chariot drivers. At the morning watch the Lord in the pillar of fire and cloud looked down upon the Egyptian army, and threw the Egyptian army into panic. He clogged their chariot wheels so that they turned with difficulty. The Egyptians said,

Chorus Let us flee from the Israelites, for the Lord is fighting for them against Egypt.

Narrator Then the Lord said to Moses,

God Stretch out your hand over the sea, so that the waters may come back upon the Egyptians, upon their chariots and their chariot drivers.

Narrator So Moses stretched forth his hand over the sea, and at dawn the sea returned to its normal depth. As the Egyptians fled before it, the Lord tossed the Egyptians into the sea. The waters returned and covered the chariots and the chariot drivers, the entire army of Pharaoh that followed them into the sea; not one of them remained. But Israelites walked on dry ground through the sea, the waters forming a wall for them on their right hand and on their left. Thus the Lord saved Israel that day from the hands of the Egyptians.

Collect

Lord God our redeemer, who heard the cry of your people
and sent your servant Moses to lead them out of slavery:
free us from the tyranny of sin and death and,
by the leading of your Spirit, bring us to our promised land;
through Jesus Christ our Lord.

Common Worship, Times and Seasons p.382

Music

When Israel was in Egypt's land *or* The Lord's my shepherd

From death to life *Ezekiel 37:1–14*

Ezekiel The hand of the Lord came upon me, and he brought me out by the Spirit of the Lord, and set me down in the middle of a valley; it was full of bones. He led me all around them, there were very many lying in the valley, and they were very dry. He said to me,

God Mortal, can these bones live?

Ezekiel O Lord God, you know.

God Prophesy to these bones and say to them, O dry bones hear the word of the Lord. Thus says the Lord God to these bones, I will cause breath to enter you, and you shall live. I will lay sinews on you, and will cause flesh to come upon you, and cover you with skin, and put breath in you and you shall live. You shall know that I am the Lord.

Ezekiel So, I prophesied as I had been commanded; and as I prophesied, there was a noise and a rattling, and the bones came together, bone to its bone. I looked, and there were sinews on them, and flesh had come upon them, and skin had covered them; but there was no breath in them. Then he said to me,

God Prophesy to the breath, prophesy, mortal, and say to the breath, Thus says the Lord God: Come from the four winds, O breath and breathe upon these slain, that they may live.

Ezekiel I prophesied as he commanded me and breath came into them, and they lived, and stood on their feet, a vast multitude. Then he said to me,

God Mortal, these bones are the whole house of Israel. They say,

Chorus Our bones are dried up, and our hope is lost; we are cut off completely.

God Therefore prophesy and say to them, Thus says the Lord God: I am going to open your graves and raise you up from your graves, and I will bring you back to the land of Israel. And you shall know that I am the Lord, when I open your graves, and bring you up from your graves, O my people. I will put my spirit within you, and you shall live, and I will place you on your own soil; then you shall know that I, the Lord, have spoken and will act, says the Lord.

Collect

Blessed are you, Lord God of our salvation.
You bring life from the darkest valley of death.
When hope is lost and our dry bones are scattered in shame,
speak your word to your broken people, that we may stand
confidently before you, and breathe your Spirit into us that we
might live, O Lord, our maker and redeemer.

Common Worship, Times and Seasons p.390

Music

O Lord my God (How great thou art)

The vigil continues with:

The service of light

There is now a procession out of the darkened church to where the Easter fire is to be lit. Easter fire awaits us like Christ waits upon us to welcome him.

Hymn

Sing this at the fire as it is lit. If a fire is not possible, a charcoal fire can easily be lit in a tray.

Christ as a light *(or the first two verses and chorus of* Lord, the light of your love is shining*)*

The Easter Fire is blessed

Eternal God,
who made this most holy night
to shine with the brightness of your one true light:
make this new fire holy
and set us aflame with the fire of your love,
and bring us to the radiance of your heavenly glory;
through Christ our Lord.

The Easter Candle is blessed

Christ yesterday and today, the beginning and the end,
Alpha and Omega, all time belongs to him,
and all ages,

to him be glory and power
through every age and for ever.
Amen.

At the placing of the studs in the candle to represent the wounds of Christ
By his holy and glorious wounds,
may Christ our Lord guard and keep us.
Amen.

The Easter Candle is lit from the fire with the words
May the light of Christ, rising in glory,
banish all darkness from our hearts.

The candle is raised high with the words
The Light of Christ, Alleluia, Alleluia.
Thanks be to God, Alleluia, Alleluia.

We now return to church with the paschal candle carried before us.

Hymns
To be sung on the way back into church.
Walk in the light
Rejoice in the Lord always
Jubilate, Deo

On entering the church, whoever is carrying the candle proclaims
The Light of Christ.
Thanks be to God.

In church, it is good for everyone to light a small candle from the Easter Candle or from a friend's candle lit from the Easter Candle. When all candles are lit and the Easter Candle is in place, let all hold their candles high and repeat the words.

The Light of Christ.
Thanks be to God.

Alleluia, Christ is risen.
He is risen indeed, Alleluia.

The Gospel
Matthew 28:1–10

After the Gospel is announced, but before it is read, sing Alleluias.
('Celtic Alleluia' by Fintan O'Carroll or the Alleluia from 'Seek ye first the kingdom of God')

After the Gospel has been read:

We are Easter people;
Alleluia is our song.

Repeat the Alleluias sung before the Gospel.

Collect
Lord God, giver of life and hope,
through the glorious resurrection of your Son,
death and hell are defeated
and you have opened for us the way to everlasting life.
Grant that we may know Christ and the power of his resurrection,
and so rejoice in the fullness of life which is eternal;
we ask this in the name of Jesus our risen Lord.

Blessing

May you find in Christ the risen Lord,
a companion for all your journeys,
a present help in trouble,
a light in times of darkness,
and the assurance that life is eternal:
and the blessing of God Almighty, the Father,
the Son and the Holy Spirit be upon you
and remain with you always.
Amen.

Easter Day

Begin in the dark. If the room is not dark, close your eyes.

Welcome the light

Today we give thanks, for in dying Christ has conquered death; in rising to life again he has opened to us the way to everlasting life. He has been raised from the dead, and indeed he is going ahead of you.

Matthew 28:7

As we meet in the love and light of the Father, the Son and the Holy Spirit, let us rejoice in the power of the resurrection.

Alleluia, Christ is risen.
He is risen indeed, Alleluia.

The Lord is here.
His Spirit is with us.

Candle-lighting

May Christ, risen in glory, scatter the darkness from our hearts and minds and from this world.
The light of the risen Christ shine upon us, this day and always.

Alleluia, Christ is risen.
He is risen indeed, Alleluia.

Light the candle.

Blessed are you, the God and Father of our Lord Jesus Christ; to you be glory and praise for ever. By raising your Son from the dead, death has been destroyed and new life has been restored. In him the victory over sin and the grave is won. May we live as 'Easter people', reflecting the glory of your resurrection. Blessed are you Father, Son and Holy Spirit.

Reading
Matthew 28:1–10

Hymn
Jesus lives! thy terrors now *(first two verses)*

Special intention – in the light of God

Risen Lord, we remember all who walk in darkness and who are burdened with troubles, the heavy-hearted and the sad. We ask your blessing upon all who are separated from their loved ones and who feel lonely or lost. We bring before you all who are ill and all who are fearful. We ask you to comfort all who stand by a graveside weeping, and all who mourn.
Risen Lord, make your presence known to us:
you are our light and our salvation. Alleluia.

Risen Lord, we ask that we might share in your resurrection and triumph over darkness and death. We ask your blessing upon our friends and loved ones who are departed from us. May they know of your power in the fullness of your kingdom. This day we rejoice that death is conquered: we are free, for you have won the victory.
Risen Lord, make your presence known to us:
you are our light and our salvation. Alleluia.

Closing prayer

Christ, you are risen from the dead.
We are risen with you.
May our life never deny this eternal life,
this peace and hope and joy.
Praise and glory to the God of life
who is stronger than all kinds of death. Alleluia.
A New Zealand Prayer Book

Extinguish candle.

We are Easter people;
alleluia is our song.

Easter Garden

Affirmation of God's presence

Affirmation

Today we give thanks that, in dying, Christ has conquered death: in rising to life again he has opened to us the way to everlasting life.

Invitation to worship

As we meet in the love and light of the Father, the Son and the Holy Spirit, let us rejoice in the power of the resurrection.

Alleluia Christ is risen.
He is risen indeed, Alleluia.

The Lord is here.
His Spirit is with us.

Hymn

Jesus, stand among us

Silence

Candle-lighting

Prayer

At the lighting of the Easter Candle.
May Christ, risen in glory,
scatter the darkness from our hearts and minds and from this world.
The light of the risen Christ shine upon us, this day and always.

Alleluia, Christ is risen.
He is risen indeed, Alleluia.

Blessed are you, the God and Father of our Lord Jesus Christ; to you be glory and praise for ever. By raising your Son from the dead, death has been destroyed and new life has been restored. In him the victory over sin and the grave is won. May we live as 'Easter people'

reflecting the glory of your resurrection. Blessed are you Father, Son and Holy Spirit.
Silence

Hymn
Low in the grave he lay

Night of doubt and sorrow *Or read John 19:40–42*

Mary It is another restless night of red eyes and tears, a long, sleepless night. It is another night when the darkness seems to go on for ever. Sleep will not come. If only I could go to sleep and not wake up again: it would be better. To end it all and to be with him, for when he died something in me died also.

There are times when the dawn never comes. The psalmist said, 'Heaviness may endure for a night, but joy comes in the morning.' It may have been so for him but for me today will be like yesterday – empty and painful. His presence has gone out of my life, everything is an effort, all is dark. It would be easy to give up.

This heaviness I feel is like a great weight, a stone rolled onto my heart as the stone rolled against the tomb. There is such a weight on my mind, that has been rolled into my life. It began only two days ago, on Friday. I saw him die . . . I saw his agony . . . He was left alone by his friends. He was tortured: he was crucified. He was such a good man. Where is the justice of this? Why do the good often suffer? Why? . . . Why? . . . Why? That was his cry from the cross and there was no answer then. It made me weep and turned my heart to stone.

Who can answer this?

Who can lift the stone?

The great weight, which oppresses me, who can lift it?

If only I could go to Jesus.

If someone would roll the stone away I would go to him.

I would care for his lifeless body and show that I still love him.

It is always darkest before the dawn. I cannot sit still. I will go to where they have laid him.

I will go to Jesus. I will get as close as I can.

If only someone would roll the stone away. Please God help me!

Let someone roll the stone away.

Prayer

Blessed are you, Jesus Christ our risen Lord,
for out of your love you drew Mary to your tomb, to be with you:
and in that love you placed her where she would experience the glory of your resurrection.
Blessed are you, risen Lord, with the Father and the holy Spirit one God for ever and ever.
Amen.

Hymn

The angel rolled the stone away
At this point a child could roll to the side the stone at the tomb.

Day of resurrection *Or read John 20:1, 2, 14b–18*

Mary What has been going on while I have been in the dark? Someone has been at work, someone with great strength. The stone has been moved, it must have taken a great power to do that.

I will go and see my Lord. Already I feel as if the clouds are lifting and the stone is rolled away. A great weight has been lifted from my heart and my mind.

Oh, no! They have taken away my Lord: they have carried him off.

Oh Jesus, where are you?

Oh Lord, what have they done? I do not know where they have laid him.

Where can he be? How cruel, I need him. I need his presence.

I cannot live without him. Where is he?!

I must get a grip of myself. I cannot see straight for tears.

My vision is blurred: my heart aches.

There is someone over there. Is it the gardener? He seems to be looking at the spring flowers which have just burst through the earth. I will ask him. Sir, they have taken away my Lord. Do you know . . .

Jesus Mary.

Mary No it can't be. Is it really him? This is madness.

Is it really you my Lord? Is it you?

Jesus Mary.

Mary Master! Master! Let me stay here with you. Let me touch you. I want to stay close to you and hug you, to love you and stay with you for ever.

Jesus Mary, do not cling to me. You will have to let me go.

Mary, you cannot keep me to yourself.

Go, Mary. Yes, I know it is hard. Go Mary, go and tell the others. Tell the disciples the Good News I am risen. I am alive. Let them come out of the darkness in to the light. Let them discover this is a new day and a new world. Tell them you have seen the Lord.

Mary I have seen the Lord. Alleluia!

Prayer

Blessed are you risen Lord,
you have conquered death with your resurrection:
you have triumphed over hatred with your love:
you have restored to us the hope of eternal life.
Blessed are you risen Lord, with the Father and the Holy Spirit,
one God for ever and ever.
Amen.

Hymn

Jesus Christ is risen today

During the hymn, a single candle is lit to represent Mary seeing the risen Lord.

The Lord is risen indeed *Or read John 20:3–10*

Peter I haven't cried for years. I don't like to see grown men cry. But the tears have flowed these last two days. I am so ashamed of myself. I have never done anything so bad as this. I will never forgive myself. How can I? I have denied Jesus. I have said I do not believe in him: that I am not one of his disciples, that I do not follow him. Where can I go? For only he makes sense of the world: only through him has my life purpose and meaning. That was before Friday. It was the way he looked at me before he died. He looked so heartbroken, so full of sorrow. I felt it was my fault. He had heard it all. I had denied him: not once, not twice, but three times. Three times I tried to hide. Three times I lacked courage. Three times I said I am not his disciple.

Mary Peter, Peter, I have seen the Lord!

Peter Mary, what are you saying? Jesus is crucified, dead and buried. What madness is this?

Mary The greatest madness of all, he is alive. I met him in the garden. I have seen the Lord, Alleluia!

Peter What do you make of this, John? I can hardly make sense of Mary. I think we had better go and see for ourselves what is going on.

So we ran, John and I, to the tomb. I am not as swift as I used to be and young John outran me. When he got there the stone was rolled away and he did not dare go into the tomb. When I got there we went in. We saw the grave clothes but there was no body. It was the way the clothes were wrapped that was so strange: it was as if he had come through them!

Pause

We did not understand it then. How could we? We just could not take it in. It was later he came to us. He is alive! He spoke to us. He shared a meal with us. He spoke especially to me. It sounds silly but I nearly got angry with him! He asked the same question over and over.

Jesus Peter, do you really love me?

Peter He knew the answer. He knew I loved him. Yet he asked me three times. I answered, 'Yes. Yes, yes of course I do!' Three times and then I had lost my guilt: I knew he had forgiven me. He is alive and is offering me newness of life, he seeks me as his friend.

I have seen the Lord. Alleluia.

Prayer

Blessed are you risen Lord,
for through the empty grave you challenge your disciples,
you brought them to think about you and talk about you
and in your love you drew them towards you.
Lord, draw us with the cords of love to know you are risen indeed.
Blessed are you, risen Lord, with the Father and the Holy Spirit,
one God for ever and ever.
Amen.

Hymn

Alleluia! Give thanks to the risen Lord
During the hymn, two candles are lit to represent Peter and John seeing the risen Lord.

Abide with us, Lord *Or read Luke 24:13–35*

Cleopas We had turned our backs on Jerusalem. It was late in the day and we were walking towards the setting sun: the sun that set on all our dreams and hopes. We were going west: the sunset road. We were going into the dark. That is just the way we thought our lives were going. Our world had fallen apart, it all seemed hopeless and meaningless.

We turned our backs on Jerusalem. Cities can be such hard and cruel places: the politicians were corrupt, injustice was rife. People were out for themselves. It was the cruelty of Jesus' death that sickened us: faith and hope seemed to die with him.

We turned our backs on the Church leaders: they were no better than the politicians. You could say we were disillusioned, disenchanted. We had hoped, but . . .

We had hoped that Jesus would make a difference.

We had hoped that he would show us a new way of living.

We had hoped that he was the Christ.

We had hoped, but we saw him die: and our hopes and dreams died with him.

We have lost hope, so we are going west, the setting of the sun and the setting of life.

We were like all people going into the dark, into the unknown.

It was then he came!

He came to us.

He walked with us.

He talked to us.

He came and stayed with us.

It was when he took the bread at supper time the clouds seemed to lift; the room had a strange feel to it.

He took the bread and broke it and our broken hearts were mended.

We were in no doubt at all. It was the Lord!

We knew him in the breaking of the bread. He quietly said, 'Take, eat' and broke it.

Do this in remembrance. Remember me, I am with you always.

Remember to the end of time.

Our hearts soared on high.

We have seen the Lord. Alleluia.

Collect

Blessed are you, risen Lord,
for you are ever with us as our companion and friend:
you walk with us, you are ready to talk with us,
you abide with us.
May our hearts burn with longing for you and your salvation.
Blessed are you, risen Lord, with the Father and the Holy Spirit,
one God for ever and ever.
Amen.

Hymn

Jesus lives!
During the hymn two candles are lit to represent Cleopas and companion seeing the risen Lord.

Peace be with you *Or read John 20:19–23*

Disciple There are times when you need to run away: times when you can take no more. You lock your doors to keep trouble out.

You shutter your windows, close your eyes and lie low.

You know you have had enough.

For a time I felt there was no problem too big to run away from.

We bolted the doors and blocked the windows.

It was so dark it was like being in a tomb.

We might as well have died with Jesus as be buried alive in this place.

We had locked our hearts against feeling: and our minds to all thought, or so we thought.

Many of our fears and troubles were locked in with us.

You cannot run away from life or from yourself.

We were fearful, anxious, restricted.

We hardly dared move. Then he came.

I cannot explain it at all. I only know it happened.

No one opened the door. No one moved but he was there with us.

He came to us. He breathed life into us.

He burst into our prison and broke us out of it. He set us free.

He came to our troubles with his joy.

He came to our darkness with his light.

He dispersed our fears with his love.

He came to us as if he had never been away. He said,

Jesus Peace be with you. Peace, the deep, deep peace of God be within you.

Do not let your hearts be troubled. Believe in God: believe in me.

Peace, my peace, I give to you. My peace I leave with you.

A peace like the world cannot give I give to you.

Disciple Then he came to each of us individually. He touched us.

He breathed new life into us.

It was like being newly created.

We felt his risen power in each of us.

Because he lives we live also.

He is with us always.

I have seen the Lord. Alleluia.

Hymn

Peace is flowing like a river

During the hymn, eight candles are lit to represent the disciples who saw the risen Lord. We already have candles for Peter and John, Thomas is missing and Judas Iscariot is no more.

My Lord and my God *Or read John 20:24–31*

Thomas You don't want to believe all you hear. Some people are right storytellers.

Can you believe what you have heard tonight?

That Jesus is alive and to be met, I doubt it.

You should not accept these things just because you are told them: you should test them for yourself.

They tried it on me. They said that Jesus is alive, that they walked with him and talked with him.

I know better for I had seen him die. I saw his burial: and when you're dead, you're dead. Though, I remember the raising of the son of the widow at Nain: I was outside when he raised the daughter of Jairus: I was present at the raising of Lazarus. But really when you're dead that's it.

That is why I went away to the country. I wanted to be safe, to hide until it was all quiet again. I went to my twin brother's.

Yet when I came back to Jerusalem the others were so excited, they were saying they had seen Jesus, that he is alive. Me, I doubt it.

Mary's a great lass, but she is a bit hysterical. She's been overwrought. She said she found the tomb empty. I think she could well have gone to the wrong place. As for seeing the Lord – well I ask you! But the ten disciples insisted they had seen him. I thought better of Peter and the other fishermen; I thought they were all so level-headed. Yet they have all been through a lot. Still they insist they have seen him. If it is true, life could never be the same again. I will only believe if I can see him for myself; if I can put my fingers in the nail holes and know it is him. If I can thrust my fist into his wounded side then I will believe. I will not believe unless I can see, can touch, can experience for myself.

Jesus Thomas! *Pause* Thomas!

Thomas Oh my Lord.

Jesus Thomas.

Thomas Oh my God.

Jesus Thomas, do not be unbelieving. Come close to me. Put your hand in mine. Come, put your fist into my side. Look and feel and know it is I and I am real. You now see because you believe, blessed are those who have not seen me but who yet believe.

Thomas I have seen the Lord, Alleluia!

Prayer

Blessed are you risen Lord, for you came to Thomas in his doubting and you revealed to him your wounded hands and side. Lord, in our doubts and darkness you are there. You do not leave us or forsake us. Open our eyes to your presence and our hearts to your love, that we may know you as our Lord and our God. Blessed are you, risen Lord, with the Father and the Holy Spirit, one God for ever and ever. **Amen.**

Hymn

Alleluia (x8)

During the hymn, a candle is lit for Thomas.

Reading

Romans 8:35–39

The Lord's Prayer

Litany

Risen Lord, you were known to Mary in the garden,
be present with us and set our hearts on fire with love for you.

Risen Lord, you came to your disciples who met behind closed doors,
be present with us and set our hearts on fire with love for you.

Risen Lord, you walked with Cleopas and his companion on the road,
be present with us and set our hearts on fire with love for you.

Risen Lord, you showed yourself to doubting Thomas,
be present with us and set our hearts on fire with love for you.

Risen Lord, you appeared to the disciples by the Sea of Galilee,
be present with us and set our hearts on fire with love for you.

There is still one more candle to add those who know the risen Lord. This candle is for you.

As the candle is lit, sing the hymn.

Hymn
Thine be the glory

Prayer
May the light of your presence, risen Lord, set our hearts on fire with love for you that we may live to your praise and glory.

Silence

Blessing

May you find in Christ the risen Lord
a sure ground for your faith,
a firm support for your hopes,
the assurance of love everlasting,
the promise of life eternal,
and the blessing of God Almighty, the Father, the Son
and the Holy Spirit,
be upon you and your loved ones, now and evermore.
Amen.

Easter 2
The risen Lord and Mary

Affirmation of God's presence

Affirmation

Today we give thanks that, in dying, Christ has conquered death: in rising to life again he has opened to us the way to everlasting life. As the risen Lord was seen by Mary, may he also be known to us.

Invitation to worship

As we meet in the love and light of the Father, the Son and the Holy Spirit, let us rejoice in the power of the resurrection.

Alleluia Christ is risen.
He is risen indeed, Alleluia.

The Lord is here.
His Spirit is with us.

Hymn

Love's redeeming work is done

Silence

Candle-lighting

Prayer

At the lighting of the Easter Candle.

May Christ, risen in glory, scatter the darkness from our hearts and minds and from this world. The light of the risen Christ shine upon us this day and always.

Alleluia, Christ is risen.
He is risen indeed, Alleluia.

Blessed are you, the God and Father of our Lord Jesus Christ, to you be glory and praise for ever. By raising your Son from the dead, death has been destroyed and new life has been restored. In him the victory over sin and the grave is won. We rejoice that you, risen Lord, appeared to Mary in the garden, transforming her sorrow into joy, that you sent her to your disciples to proclaim you are risen. May our lives reflect the glory of your resurrection. Blessed are you Father, Son and Holy Spirit.

Silence

Ministry of the Word

Old Testament
The Song of Solomon 3:1–4

Hymn
The angel rolled the stone away

The Gospel
John 19:41–20:18

After the Gospel is announced, but before it is read, sing Alleluias.
('Celtic Alleluia' by Fintan O'Carroll or the Alleluia from 'Seek ye first the kingdom of God')

After the Gospel has been read, let a woman light a candle from the Easter Candle and say:

I light this candle for Mary Magdalene who met the risen Lord in the garden.
We are Easter people;
Alleluia is our song.

Repeat the Alleluias sung before the Gospel.

Sermon

Silence

Hymn
Walking in the garden

Response

Creed

Confession

Thanksgiving
Holy and ever-living God, we give you thanks and praise that Christ is risen. In dying he has conquered death and in rising again has opened for us the way to life eternal. Today we give you thanks that in turning away from the tomb Mary met you, the risen Lord. The heaviness of her heart was rolled away in the joy of your presence. May our lives reflect the joy and the glory of the resurrection and may we live to praise you, Lord and giver of life eternal. **Amen.**

Intercessions
Lord, make us aware of your risen presence in our lives that our worship may be full of joy and awe. Give us the courage to go out and to proclaim your love and your saving power. Lord, as we rejoice in your resurrection, we ask your blessing upon all who celebrate your presence, all who know you as the risen Lord. We pray for all who seek you and all who want to be close to you. Risen Lord, strengthen your Church to tell the Good News to the whole world.
Risen Lord, make your presence known to us.
You are our light and our salvation.

Lord Jesus, as we rejoice in your risen presence, we remember peoples and nations that long for peace and renewal. We ask your blessing upon all who live in life-threatening places, who suffer from poverty or from war, all who are deprived or terrorised. May they find new ways to heal their divisions and new ways that lead to a fuller and richer life. May they find in you their peace. Risen Lord, make your presence known to us.
You are our light and our salvation.

Risen Lord, you appeared to Mary; may we know your presence in our homes and in all our dealings. Let us walk and work in your presence and seek to reveal your glory in the world. We ask you to bless all our loved ones and friends and keep us ever in your love.
Risen Lord, make your presence known to us.
You are our light and our salvation.

Risen Lord, we remember all who walk in darkness and who are burdened with troubles, the heavy-hearted and the sad. We ask your blessing upon all who are separated from their loved ones and who feel lonely or lost. We bring before you all who are ill and all who are fearful. We ask you to comfort all who stand by a graveside weeping, and all who mourn.
Risen Lord, make your presence known to us.
You are our light and our salvation.

Risen Lord, we ask that we might share in your resurrection and triumph over darkness and death. We ask your blessing upon our friends and loved ones who are departed from us. May they know of your power in the fullness of your kingdom. This day we rejoice that death is conquered: we are free, for you have won the victory.
Alleluia.
Merciful Father,
accept these prayers for the sake of your Son,
our Saviour Jesus Christ.
Amen.

Collect

Glory and honour and blessing be yours,
great and mighty God, in the resurrection you have destroyed death
and opened to us the gate of glory.
In you, O Christ, are life and life eternal.
As you appeared to Mary,
may you also be known to us in your risen power.
We give you thanks and praise risen Lord,
with the Father and the Holy Spirit,
one God for ever and ever.
Amen.

The Lord's Prayer

Silence

Hymn
Now the green blade riseth

Blessing

May you know in your life the power
and the presence of the risen Lord, let his love and light fill you:
and the blessing of God Almighty,
the Father, the Son and the Holy Spirit
be upon you this day and for evermore.
Amen.

Easter 2
Rejoice in the Lord

Begin in the dark. If the room is not dark, close your eyes.

Welcome the light

Today we give thanks, for in dying Christ has conquered death; in rising to life again he has opened to us the way to everlasting life. She turned round and saw Jesus standing there, but she did not know it was Jesus.

John 20:14

As we meet in the love and light of the Father, the Son and the Holy Spirit, let us rejoice in the power of the resurrection.

Alleluia, Christ is risen.
He is risen indeed, Alleluia.

The Lord is here.
His Spirit is with us.

Candle-lighting

May Christ, risen in glory, scatter the darkness from our hearts and minds and from this world.
The light of the risen Christ shine upon us, this day and always.

Alleluia, Christ is risen.
He is risen indeed, Alleluia.

Light the candle.

Blessed are you, the God and Father of our Lord Jesus Christ; to you be glory and praise for ever. By your raising your Son from the dead, death has been destroyed and new life has been restored. In him the victory over sin and the grave is won. We rejoice that you, risen Lord, appeared to Mary in the garden, transforming her sorrow into joy, that you sent her to your disciples to proclaim you are risen. May our lives reflect the glory of your resurrection. Blessed are you Father, Son and Holy Spirit.

Reading
John 19:41–20:18

Hymn
All in an Easter garden

Special intention – in the light of God

Lord, make us aware of your risen presence. Roll away the heaviness, the doubt, the fear from our hearts. Fill our lives with the knowledge of your presence and your love, that our whole being may rejoice. Give us the courage to go out and to proclaim your love and your saving power. Lord, as we rejoice in your resurrection, we ask your blessing upon all who celebrate your presence, all who know you as the risen Lord. We pray for all who seek you and all who want to be close to you. Risen Lord, strengthen your Church to tell the Good News to the whole world.
Risen Lord, make your presence known to us:
you are our light and our salvation. Alleluia.

Risen Lord, as you appeared to Mary, may we know your presence in our homes and in all our dealings. Let us walk and work in your presence and seek to reveal your glory in the world. We ask you to bless all our loved ones and friends and keep us all ever in your love and in the power of your resurrection.
Risen Lord, make your presence known to us:
you are our light and our salvation.

Closing prayer

The whole bright world rejoices now:
with laughing cheer! with boundless joy!
The birds do sing on every bough:
Alleluia.

Then shout beneath the racing skies:
with laughing cheer! with boundless joy!
To him who rose that we might rise:
Alleluia.

Easter carol, 17th century

Extinguish candle.

We are Easter people;
alleluia is our song.

Easter 3
The risen Lord and the ten disciples

Affirmation of God's presence

Affirmation

Today, we give thanks that, in dying, Christ has conquered death: in rising to life again he has opened to us the way to everlasting life. As the risen Lord appeared to his disciples, let us know he is with us.

Invitation to worship

As we meet in the grace and glory of the Father, the Son and the Holy Spirit, we rejoice in the presence of the risen Lord and the power of his resurrection.

Alleluia Christ is risen.
He is risen indeed, Alleluia.

The Lord is here.
His Spirit is with us.

Hymn

Jesus, stand among us

Silence

Candle-lighting

Prayer

At the lighting of the Easter Candle.

May Christ, risen in glory, scatter the darkness from our hearts and minds and from this world. The light of the risen Christ shine upon us this day and always. Blessed are you, Lord God, by whose power our Lord Jesus is raised from the dead. In your presence is life and life eternal. In your power death is conquered and the gate to eternal life is opened. We rejoice that you appeared to the disciples in the Upper

Room and that in your presence is the fullness of joy. Blessed are you Father, Son and Holy Spirit.

Silence

Ministry of the Word

Old Testament
Isaiah 43:1–3a, 10–12

Hymn
Jesus lives! thy terrors now

The Gospel
John 20:19–23

After the Gospel is announced, but before it is read, sing Alleluias.
('Celtic Alleluia' by Fintan O'Carroll or the Alleluia from 'Seek ye first the kingdom of God')

After the Gospel has been read, have ten people light candles from the Easter candle then let them say:

We light these ten candles for the disciples to whom the risen Christ appeared.

Alleluia, Christ is risen.
He is risen indeed, Alleluia.

We are Easter people;
Alleluia is our song.

Repeat the Alleluias sung before the Gospel.

Sermon

Silence

Hymn

Breathe on me, breath of God

Response

Creed

Confession

Thanksgiving

Holy and ever-living God, we give you thanks and praise that Christ is risen. In dying he has conquered death and in rising again has opened for us the way to life eternal. Today we rejoice that you, Lord Christ, appeared to the disciples in an ordinary home. You filled their hearts with joy and breathed new life into them giving them courage and hope to go out and proclaim that you have triumphed over death. We give you thanks for all who have witness to you and the power of your resurrection. Glory to you risen Christ, with the Father and the Holy Spirit, one God now and for ever. **Amen.**

Intercessions

Risen Lord, come and stand among us that we may know you and love you, that we may love you and worship you, that we may worship you and serve you today and always. Grant to your Church the power to proclaim your salvation and the joy of your resurrection. Bless all who quietly wait upon you in prayer and meditation. Empower your priests and ministers to reveal your love and your presence. Grant, O risen Lord, that we all may witness to you as our Lord and Saviour.
Lord of life, hear us
and grant us your peace.

Risen Lord, may the world know your peace: may it rise above divisions and strife that your victory over darkness and death may be known to all. We remember before you all who are closed in by poverty or fear, all who are imprisoned and all who are captive to their own vices and addictions. Lord, may they know that you come to set the prisoner free.
Lord of life, hear us
and grant us your peace.

Risen Lord, as you came to the disciples in an ordinary home, be known in our homes.
Come risen Lord, be known among us and our loved ones:
come, enter our darkness and fears with your light:
come, break into all that would imprison us and set us free:
come to our fear of venturing
and send us out in the power of your Spirit.
Lord of life, hear us
and grant us your peace.

Risen Lord, we remember in your presence all who are housebound and all whose lives are restricted through their surroundings. We ask your blessing upon all who are suffering from depression or anxiety, all who are awaiting operations or a doctor's diagnosis. We pray for all who are not at peace with themselves, their neighbours or with you. May we all in our weakness know of your love and saving power.
Lord of life, hear us
and grant us your peace.

Risen Lord, giver of life eternal, we ask your blessing upon our loved ones departed. May they rejoice in the fullness of your kingdom and in your peace.
Merciful Father,
accept these prayers for the sake of your Son,
our Saviour Jesus Christ.
Amen.

Collect

Lord Christ, Prince of peace, as you appeared to your disciples in the closed room come into our lives:
breathe into us your life-giving Spirit:
grant us your peace: empower us to witness to your resurrection and that you are with us.
We ask this, for you are alive and live and reign
with the Father and the Holy Spirit, one God for ever and ever.
Amen.

The Lord's Prayer

Silence

Hymn
Lord Jesus Christ, you have come to us

Blessing

The peace of the risen Christ,
the peace which the world cannot give,
the peace which passes all understanding,
the peace of him who triumphed over death, be yours:
and the blessing of God Almighty,
the Father, the Son and the Holy Spirit
be upon you and remain with you always.
Amen.

Easter 3
The peace of the risen Lord

Begin in the dark. If the room is not dark, close your eyes.

Welcome the light

Today we give thanks, for in dying Christ has conquered death; in rising to life again he has opened to us the way to everlasting life. The disciples rejoiced when they saw the Lord.

John 20:20

As we meet in the love and light of the Father, the Son and the Holy Spirit, let us rejoice in the power of the resurrection.

Alleluia, Christ is risen.
He is risen indeed, Alleluia.

The Lord is here.
His Spirit is with us.

Candle-lighting

May Christ, risen in glory, scatter the darkness from our hearts and minds and from this world.
The light of the risen Christ shine upon us, this day and always.

Alleluia, Christ is risen.
He is risen indeed, Alleluia.

Light the candle.

Blessed are you, Lord God, by whose power our Lord Jesus is raised from the dead. In your presence is life and life eternal. In your power, death is conquered and the gate to eternal life is open. We rejoice that you appeared to the disciples in the upper room and that in your presence is the fullness of joy. Blessed are you Father, Son and Holy Spirit.

Reading
John 20:19–23

Hymn
Jesus, stand among us in thy risen power

Special intention – in the light of God

Risen Lord, come stand among us that we may know you and love you, that we may love you and worship you, that we may worship you and serve you today and always.
Risen Lord, as you came to the disciples in an ordinary home, be known in our homes.
Come, risen Lord; be known among us and our loved ones:
come, enter our darkness and fears with your light:
come, break into all that would imprison us and set us free:
come, to our fear of venturing, and send us out in the power of your Spirit.
Lord of life eternal, hear us
and grant us your peace.

Risen Lord, we remember in your presence all who are housebound and all whose lives are restricted through their surroundings. We ask your blessing upon all who are suffering from depression or anxiety, all who are awaiting operations or a doctor's diagnosis. We pray for all who are not at peace with themselves, their neighbours or with you. May we all in our weakness know of your love and saving power.
Lord of life eternal, hear us
and grant us your peace.

Closing prayer

Risen Christ, Prince of Peace, come among us.
As you appeared to your disciples in the closed room,
come into our lives.
Come, breathe into us your life-giving Spirit.
Come, grant us your peace.
Come, empower us to witness to your resurrection.

Come and be known among us.
We ask this for you are alive
and live and reign with the Father
and the Holy Spirit, one God for ever and ever.
Amen.

Extinguish candle.

We are Easter people;
alleluia is our song.

Easter 4
The risen Lord and Thomas

Affirmation of God's presence

Affirmation

Today we give thanks that, in dying, Christ has conquered death: in rising to life again he has opened to us the way to everlasting life. As the risen Lord came to Thomas, even in his doubting, let us know that he comes to us now.

Invitation to worship

As we meet in the presence and power of the Father, the Son and the Holy Spirit, let us rejoice in the glory of the resurrection.

Alleluia Christ is risen.
He is risen indeed, Alleluia.

The Lord is here.
His Spirit is with us.

Hymn

This is the day

Silence

Candle-lighting

Prayer

At the lighting of the Easter Candle.

May Christ, risen in glory, scatter the darkness from our hearts and minds and from this world. The light of the risen Christ shine upon us this day and always. Blessed are you, our Lord and God, for out of your love you have made all things. You come to us and give yourself to us, even though we may doubt you. Help us to be aware of you in our lives and to give ourselves to you in love and in doing your will. Blessed are you Father, Son and Holy Spirit.

Silence

Ministry of the Word

Old Testament
Job 19:23–27a

Hymn
O let the Son of God enfold you

The Gospel
John 20:24–31

After the Gospel is announced, but before it is read, sing Alleluias.
('Celtic Alleluia' by Fintan O'Carroll or the Alleluias from 'Seek ye first the kingdom of God')

After the Gospel has been read, have someone light a candle from the Easter Candle then let them say:

I light this candle for Thomas to whom the risen Christ appeared amid his doubts.

Alleluia, Christ is risen.
He is risen indeed, Alleluia.

We are Easter people;
Alleluia is our song.

Repeat the Alleluias sung before the Gospel.

Sermon

Silence

Hymn
Alleluia, Alleluia, give thanks to the risen Lord

Response

Creed

Confession

Thanksgiving

Holy and ever-living God, we give you thanks and praise that Christ is risen. In dying he has conquered death and in rising again he has opened for us the way to life eternal. Today we rejoice that you, Lord Christ, appeared to Thomas though he doubted your resurrection. We give thanks that you never leave us even when we doubt you or forget you. We thank you for all your faithful people who, though they have not seen you, believe in you and reveal in their lives your risen power.
Glory to you risen Christ, with the Father and the Holy Spirit, one God now and for ever. **Amen.**

Intercessions

Risen Lord, we ask your blessing upon all your faithful people, all those who confess you as their Lord and their God. We remember all who meet in your name and talk of your power. We pray for study groups and theological colleges, for all who meditate on your word and who seek your presence. We bring before you all who are beset with doubt and disbelief and all who are reaching out to seek you, to touch you and to find you. We pray especially for the Church in India.
Lord of life, hear us
and grant us your peace.

Risen Lord, we thank you for your great love for the world. We ask your blessing upon nations and peoples. We remember all who are striving for justice and freedom, all who are spending their lives in the service of others. We pray for all who work in the relief of poverty and of oppression. We bring before you all who seek to bring peace and harmony to our world.
Lord of life, hear us
and grant us your peace.

Risen Lord, we thank you for all who have been a strength and support to us in our daily living, all who have taught us and those who have shared their joys and their faith with us. We ask your blessing upon them and upon our friends and families. We remember before you all who seek to help and aid others in their need.
Lord of life, hear us
and grant us your peace.

Risen Lord, we remember before you all who have lost confidence in themselves or in others, those who have lost vision or trust. We ask your blessing upon all who are ill, all who have been injured in accidents or by acts of violence and upon all who have the care of them. Give them courage and hope amidst their troubles.
Lord of life, hear us
and grant us your peace.

Risen Lord, may we know that in you life is eternal. We ask your blessing upon all who have served you faithfully and upon all our loved and dear ones departed. May they know you and the joys of your kingdom.
Merciful Father,
accept these prayers for the sake of your Son,
our Saviour Jesus Christ.
Amen.

Collect

Jesus, King of glory, you are our Lord and our God:
as you appeared to Thomas you come to us.
You come to our darkness with your light,
to our doubting with your presence.
In your death you have triumphed over death:
you come to us with the gift of life eternal.
Grant that by your wounded hands
and side we may know your love and your healing power.
Then Lord, in the power of your Spirit, fill us with your peace.
We ask this for your love's sake,
O Christ, who with the Father and the Holy Spirit
lives and reigns for ever.
Amen.

The Lord's Prayer

Silence

Hymn
To God be the glory!

Blessing

May you find in Christ Jesus a light in your darkness,
a living presence that dispels your doubting,
a powerful presence that fills you with peace,
a risen presence that gives you hope in all events of life:
and the blessing of God Almighty, the Father, the Son
and the Holy Spirit
be upon you and remain with you now and for ever more.
Amen.

Easter 4
The risen Lord comes to our doubts

Begin in the dark. If the room is not dark, close your eyes.

Welcome the light

Today we give thanks, for in dying Christ has conquered death; in rising to life again he has opened to us the way to everlasting life. Then he said to Thomas, 'Put your finger here and see my hands. Reach out your hand and put it in my side. Do not doubt but believe.'

John 20:27

As we meet in the love and light of the Father, the Son and the Holy Spirit, let us rejoice in the power of the resurrection.

Alleluia, Christ is risen.
He is risen indeed, Alleluia.

The Lord is here.
His Spirit is with us.

Candle-lighting

May Christ, risen in glory, scatter the darkness from our hearts and minds and from this world.
The light of the risen Christ shine upon us, this day and always.

Alleluia, Christ is risen.
He is risen indeed, Alleluia.

Light the candle.

Blessed are you, the God and Father of our Lord Jesus Christ; to you be glory and praise for ever. By the risen Lord appearing to Thomas you encourage us to wait upon you even in our doubts. You still come to us and give yourself to us, even though we may doubt you. Even when we turn away, you do not leave us. Help us to be aware of you in our lives and to give ourselves to you in love and in doing your will. Blessed are you, Father, Son and Holy Spirit.

Reading
John 20:24–31

Hymn
Love's redeeming work is done *(first two verses)*

Special intention – in the light of God

Thanksgiving
Holy and ever-living God, we give you thanks and praise that Christ is risen. In dying he has conquered death and in rising again he has opened for us the way to life eternal. Today we rejoice that you, Lord Christ, appeared to Thomas though he doubted your resurrection. We give thanks that you never leave us even when we doubt you or forget you. We thank you for all your faithful people, who, though they have not seen you, believe in you and reveal in their lives your risen power. Glory to you, risen Christ, with the Father and the Holy Spirit, one God now and for ever.
Amen.

Intercessions
Risen Lord, we ask your blessing upon all your faithful people, all those who confess you as their Lord and their God. We remember all who meet in your name and talk of your power. We pray for study groups and theological colleges, for all who meditate on your word and who seek your presence. We bring before you all who are beset by doubt and disbelief and all who are reaching out to seek you, to touch you and to find you. We pray especially for the Church in India.[1]
My Lord, and my God,
hear us and help us.

1. Tradition has it that St Thomas evangelized India.

Risen Lord, we remember before you all who have lost confidence in themselves or in others, those who have lost vision or trust. We ask your blessing upon all who are ill, all who have been injured in accidents or by acts of violence and upon all who have the care of them. Give them courage and hope amid their troubles.
Lord of life hear us
and grant us your peace.

Closing prayer

Jesus, King of glory, you are our Lord and our God:
as you appeared to Thomas, come to us.
Come to our darkness with your light,
come to our doubting with your presence.
In your death you have triumphed over death:
come to us with the gift of life-eternal.
Grant that by your wounded hands and side
we may know your love and your healing power.
Come, Lord, in the power of your Spirit,
fill us with your peace.
We ask this for your love's sake,
O Christ, who with the Father
and the Holy Spirit lives and reigns for ever.
Amen.

Extinguish candle.

We are Easter people;
alleluia is our song.

Easter 5

The risen Lord, Cleopas and companion

Affirmation of God's presence

Affirmation

Today we give thanks that, in dying, Christ has conquered death: in rising to life again he has opened to us the way to everlasting life. As the risen Lord walked and talked with Cleopas and his companion and was known to them in the breaking of the bread, let him be known to us. Let us know he abides with us and wants us to abide with him.

Invitation to worship

As we come to abide in the presence and peace of the Father, the Son and the Holy Spirit, let us rejoice in the power of the resurrection.

Alleluia, Christ is risen.
He is risen indeed, Alleluia.

The Lord is here.
His Spirit is with us.

Hymn

Be still, for the presence of the Lord

Silence

Candle-lighting

Prayer

At the lighting of the Easter Candle

May Christ, risen in glory, scatter the darkness from our hearts and minds and from this world. The light of the risen Christ shine upon us this day and always. Blessed are you, Lord Christ, for you are with us in our journeying and in our resting. You are to be found in our homes and our daily lives. You make yourself known to us in the breaking of the bread. You, Lord, are our hope and our strength: in you we trust. Blessed are you, Christ our Saviour, with the Father and Holy Spirit one God for ever and ever. **Amen.**

Silence

Ministry of the Word

Old Testament
Joshua 1:1–9

Hymn
The Lord is risen indeed

The Gospel
Luke 24:13–35

After the Gospel is announced, but before it is read, sing Alleluias.
('Celtic Alleluia' by Fintan O'Carroll or the Alleluia from 'Seek ye first the kingdom of God')

After the Gospel has been read, have two people light candles from the Easter Candle then let them say:

We light these two candles for Cleopas and his companion to whom the risen Christ appeared on the road to Emmaus.

Alleluia, Christ is risen.
He is risen indeed, Alleluia.

We are Easter people;
Alleluia is our song.

Repeat the Alleluias sung before the Gospel.

Sermon

Silence

Hymn

I am the bread of life

Response

Creed

Confession

Thanksgiving

Holy and ever-living God, we give you thanks and praise that Christ is risen. In dying he has conquered death and in rising again has opened for us the way to life eternal. Today we rejoice that you, Lord Christ, appeared to Cleopas and his companion, you walked with them, talked with them, revealed the Scriptures to them and were known to them in the breaking of the bread. In your presence their hearts were filled with joy. We thank you that you can still be known through the Scriptures and the breaking of the bread. Glory to you, risen Christ with the Father and the Holy Spirit, one God now and for ever.
Amen.

Intercessions

Risen Lord, make yourself known to us and abide with us. Travel with us as we journey through life and when our hearts are weary enlighten and encourage us. Reveal your presence to us through the Scriptures and through the sharing of meals together. Bless all who seek to tell of your presence through words or through their example. We pray for preachers and teachers of the faith and for all Christians who witness through their lives. We remember before you all who feel they are in the dark and have lost any sense or awareness of your love and presence.
Christ, with us now,
hear us and help us.

Risen Lord, make yourself known and abide with all who are making momentous journeys, all who are on the move for they have no place to call their own. We ask your blessing upon all refugees and displaced peoples, all who are caught up in war or in acts of violence or tyranny. We remember those who have lost their homes and their work through financial difficulties, all who are unemployed and who are finding life hard.
Christ, with us now,
hear us and help us.

Risen Lord, make yourself known and abide with us. When our hearts burn within us, may we know that you are near, and set our hearts on fire with love for you. Bless our homes and loved ones with a knowledge of your presence. Help us to know you are with us in all that we do and in all our relationships with others. We remember today all those who do not know of your presence, all who are lonely or feel rejected and all who feel they are missing out on life.
Christ, with us now,
hear us and help us.

Risen Lord, make yourself known to and abide with all who are broken by illness or trouble, all that can no longer cope on their own. We remember before you all who are world weary, the disillusioned and the confused; may they know you are there with them in their troubles and that you are their hope and salvation. We ask your blessing upon all who seek to relieve the sorrows and suffering of the world.
Christ, with us now,
hear us and help us.

Risen Lord, you abide with us now to eternity. We remember before you our loved ones departed and ask that they may share in the fullness of your glory. We rejoice in the fellowship of all your saints and pray that we may know with them the joy that life is eternal.
Merciful Father,
accept these prayers for the sake of your Son,
our Saviour Jesus Christ.
Amen.

Collect

Abide with us, O Lord, today and to eternity.
Abide with us in our joys and in our sorrows.
Abide with us in our success and in our failures.
Abide with us in darkness and in light.
Abide with us now and to eternity.
We ask this for your love's sake, Christ our Lord,
who lives and reigns with the Father and the Holy Spirit,
one God for ever and ever.
Amen.

The Lord's Prayer

Silence

Hymn
Abide with me

Blessing

Let the risen Christ abide in you and abide in him,
let him dwell in your heart,
let him be at home in your home,
that he may reveal in you and through you the power of his resurrection:
and the blessing of God Almighty, the Father, the Son
and the Holy Spirit
be upon you and remain with you always.
Amen.

Easter 5
The risen Lord on the road to Emmaus

Begin in the dark. If the room is not dark, close your eyes.

Welcome the light

Today we give thanks, for in dying Christ has conquered death; in rising to life again he has opened to us the way to everlasting life. Were not our hearts burning within us while he was talking to us on the road, while he was opening the scriptures to us?

Luke 24:32

As we meet in the love and light of the Father, the Son and the Holy Spirit, let us rejoice in the power of the resurrection.

Alleluia, Christ is risen.
He is risen indeed, Alleluia.

The Lord is here.
His Spirit is with us.

Candle-lighting

May Christ, risen in glory, scatter the darkness from our hearts and minds and from this world.
The light of the risen Christ shine upon us, this day and always.

Alleluia, Christ is risen.
He is risen indeed, Alleluia.

Light the candle.

Blessed are you, Lord Christ, for you are with us in our journeying and in our resting. You are to be found in our homes and our daily lives. You make yourself known to us in the breaking of the bread. you, Lord, are our hope and our strength; in you we trust. Blessed are you, Christ our Saviour, with the Father and Holy Spirit, one God for ever and ever.
Amen.

Reading
Luke 24:13–35

Hymn
Abide with me *(first verse)*

Special intention – in the light of God

We rejoice that you, Lord Christ, appeared to Cleopas and his companion; you walked with them, talked with them, revealed the Scriptures to them and were known to them in the breaking of the bread. In your presence their hearts were filled with joy. We thank you that you can still be known through the Scriptures and the breaking of the bread. Glory to you, risen Christ, with the Father and the Holy Spirit, one God now and for ever.
Amen.

Risen Lord, make yourself known to us and abide with us.
Travel with us as we journey through life.
Be known to us when our hearts are weary, and enlighten us.
Reveal your presence to us through the Scriptures
and through the sharing of meals together.
Bless all who seek to tell of your presence
through words or through their example.

We pray for preachers and teachers of the faith and for all Christians who witness through their lives. We remember before you all who feel they are in the dark and have lost any sense or awareness of your love and presence.
Christ, with us now,
hear us and help us.

Risen Lord, make yourself known
and abide with all who are making momentous journeys,
all who are on the move because they have no place to call their own.
Abide with and bless all refugees and displaced peoples,
all who are caught up in war or in acts of violence or tyranny.
Abide with those who have lost their homes and their work,
all who are unemployed and who are finding life hard.
Jesus, with us now,
abide with us and help us.

Risen Lord, make yourself known and abide with us.
Abide with us when our hearts burn within us,
may we know that you are near,
and set our hearts on fire with love for you.
Abide with all who are world-weary,
the disillusioned, and the confused;
may they know that you abide with them in their troubles
and that you are their hope and salvation.
Jesus, with us now,
abide with us and help us.

Closing prayer

Abide with us, O Lord, today and to eternity.
Abide with us in our joys and in our sorrows.
Abide with us in our success and in our failures.
Abide with us in darkness and in the light.
Abide with us in love and your salvation.
Abide with us now and to eternity.

Extinguish candle.

We are Easter people;
alleluia is our song.

Easter 6
The risen Lord on the shore

Affirmation of God's presence

Affirmation

Today, we give thanks that, in dying, Christ has conquered death and in rising to life again he has opened to us the way to everlasting life. As the risen Lord was seen by the disciples while they were fishing, let us know he is with us now and in our daily lives.

Invitation to worship

As we meet in the love and light of the Father, the Son and the Holy Spirit, let us rejoice in the power of the resurrection.

Alleluia, Christ is risen.
He is risen indeed, Alleluia.

The Lord is here.
His Spirit is with us.

Hymn

I, the Lord of sea and sky

Silence

Candle-lighting

Prayer

At the lighting of the Easter Candle.
May Christ, risen in glory, scatter the darkness from our hearts and minds and from this world. The light of the risen Christ shine upon us this day and always. Blessed are you, God and Father of our Lord Jesus Christ, to you be praise and glory for ever. Alleluia. By the raising of your Son from the dead you have opened to us the way to eternal life. As our Lord came to the disciples while they were fishing, he comes to us this day and every day, in our work, and in

our sharing together. He is to be met and to be acknowledged as our Lord. In him, you have given us an everlasting joy. Blessed are you Father, Son and Holy Spirit.

Silence

Ministry of the Word

Old Testament
Ezekiel 36:24–28

Hymn
Christ is the world in which we move

The Gospel
John 21:1–25

After the Gospel is announced, but before it is read, sing Alleluias.
('Celtic Alleluia' by Fintan O'Carroll or the Alleluia from 'Seek ye first the kingdom of God')

After the Gospel has been read, have seven people light candles from the Easter Candle, then let them say:

We light these candles for the seven disciples that met Jesus on the shore. May we meet the risen Lord on the shores of this world and the shore of eternity. May we give our love to him as he gives his love to us.

Alleluia, Christ is risen.
He is risen indeed, Alleluia.

We are Easter people;
Alleluia is our song.

Repeat the Alleluias sung before the Gospel.

Sermon

Silence

Hymn

Hark, my soul, it is the Lord

Response

Creed

Confession

Thanksgiving

Holy and ever-living God, we give you thanks and praise that Christ is risen. In dying he has conquered death and in rising again has opened for us the way to life eternal. Today we rejoice that you, Lord Christ, appeared to the disciples in their work and on the seashore. We give thanks that we can meet you in our daily routine, in our work and in our travels. We praise you for all who have met you on the shores of time and of eternity. Glory to you, risen Christ, with the Father and the Holy Spirit one God now and for ever. **Amen.**

Intercessions

Risen Lord, we rejoice that you come to us. You fill our emptiness with the glory of your presence. You call us out of darkness into the light of eternal life. As you show us your love, you ask us to follow you. May we heed your call and follow you. Empower us by your Spirit to proclaim the Good News of your salvation. Bless all who reach out to others in your name and all who you call to be shepherds of your people. We remember before you all who share in your mission to the world.
Risen Christ, ever near,
hear us and help us.

Risen Lord, we ask your blessing upon all who work hard for little gain. We remember before you all whose work is dreary, seems fruitless or meaningless. We come to you with all who are unemployed, made redundant or unable to work. We ask you to bless all who toil to provide us with our daily food and especially today we pray for fishermen and all who work upon the sea.
Risen Christ, ever near,
hear us and help us.

Risen Lord, as you love us and forgive us, help us to be loving and forgiving in our lives. Bless our homes and our relationships that they may reflect your love and reveal your presence. We ask that our community and our nation may uphold all that brings about justice and peace. We remember before you all who seek to keep law and order and all who help our communities to thrive.
Risen Christ, ever near,
hear us and help us.

Risen Lord, we ask your blessing upon all who need the healing of their memories, all who need to know your forgiveness and love. We bring before you all who suffer from past hurts or actions, may they know your power to save and give newness of life. We remember all who are finding life difficult or restricting, we pray for all who are ill or suffer from a handicap in any way. May all find in you courage and hope.
Risen Christ, ever near,
hear us and help us.

Risen Lord, you meet us on the shores of this world, and the shore of eternity. Help us to live as those who believe and trust in you and in the power of your resurrection. We ask your blessing upon all our loved ones departed; may they rejoice in your eternal glory.
Merciful Father,
accept these prayers for the sake of your Son,
our Saviour Jesus Christ.
Amen.

Collect

Praise to you King of Glory for you
revealed your risen presence to your disciples by the lakeside.
There they learnt of your love and forgiveness
and that you want them to continue to be faithful to you.
Through your power, enable us to share in your love
and forgiveness and to be known as your followers and disciples.
We ask this in your name,
O Christ, who lives and reigns with the Father and the Holy Spirit,
one God now and for ever.
Amen.

The Lord's Prayer

Silence

Hymn
Will you come and follow me

Blessing

May the risen Christ,
who fills our emptiness with his presence,
be known to you:
the power of his presence protect you:
the light of his love lead you:
the joy of the risen Christ be always with you:
and the blessing of God Almighty,
the Father, the Son and the Holy Spirit
be upon you and remain with you now and ever more.
Amen.

Easter 6
The risen Lord is always with us

Begin in the dark. If the room is not dark, close your eyes.

Welcome the light

Today we give thanks, for in dying Christ has conquered death; in rising to life again he has opened to us the way to everlasting life. Just after daybreak, Jesus stood on the beach; but the disciples did not know that it was Jesus.

John 21:4

As we meet in the love and light of the Father, the Son and the Holy Spirit, let us rejoice in the power of the resurrection.

Alleluia, Christ is risen.
He is risen indeed, Alleluia.

The Lord is here.
His Spirit is with us.

Candle-lighting

May Christ, risen in glory, scatter the darkness from our hearts and minds and from this world.
The light of the risen Christ shine upon us, this day and always.

Alleluia, Christ is risen.
He is risen indeed, Alleluia.

Light the candle.

Blessed are you God and Father of our Lord Jesus Christ, to you be praise and glory for ever. Alleluia. By the raising of your Son from the dead you have opened to us the way to eternal life. As our Lord came to the disciples while they were fishing, he comes to us this day and every day, in our work, and in our sharing together. He is to be met and to be acknowledged as our Lord. In him, you have given us an everlasting joy. Blessed are you Father, Son and Holy Spirit.

Reading

John 21:1–25

Hymn

Newness *(to the tune 'Angel Voices')*
Fishermen who toiled for nothing
on the lake all night
hear the sound of Jesus' welcome
in the morning light:
in the friendship shared at breakfast
old mistakes are lost to sight.
Every day a fresh beginning -
newness, come what may!
In the most unlikely places
Jesus reigns today;
from the past to new horizons
Christ our Saviour leads the way.
Martin E. Leckebusch

Special intention – in the light of God

Lord Jesus, we rejoice that you appeared to the disciples in their work and on the seashore. We give thanks that we can meet you in our daily routine, in our work and in our travels. We praise you for all who have met you on the shores of time and of eternity. Glory to you, risen Christ, with the Father and the Holy Spirit, one God now and for ever. **Amen.**

Risen Lord, we rejoice that you come to us.
you fill our emptiness with the glory of your presence.
you call us out of darkness into the light of eternal life.
As you show us your love, you ask us to follow you.
May we heed your call and follow you.
Risen Christ, ever near,
hear us and help us.

Risen Lord, be seen
among all who work hard for little gain,
among all whose work is dreary,
among all whose lives seem fruitless or meaningless.
Bless all who toil to provide us with our daily food,
especially fishermen and all who work upon the sea.
Risen Christ, ever near,
hear us and help us.

Closing prayer

Lord of life, come, touch our lives;
walk the borders of our world.
Come to us in our emptiness;
come with your joyfulness.
Come to us in our struggles;
come with your peace.
Come to us in our sinfulness;
come with your forgiveness.
Come Lord in time
and bring us to eternal life.

Extinguish candle.

We are Easter people;
alleluia is our song.

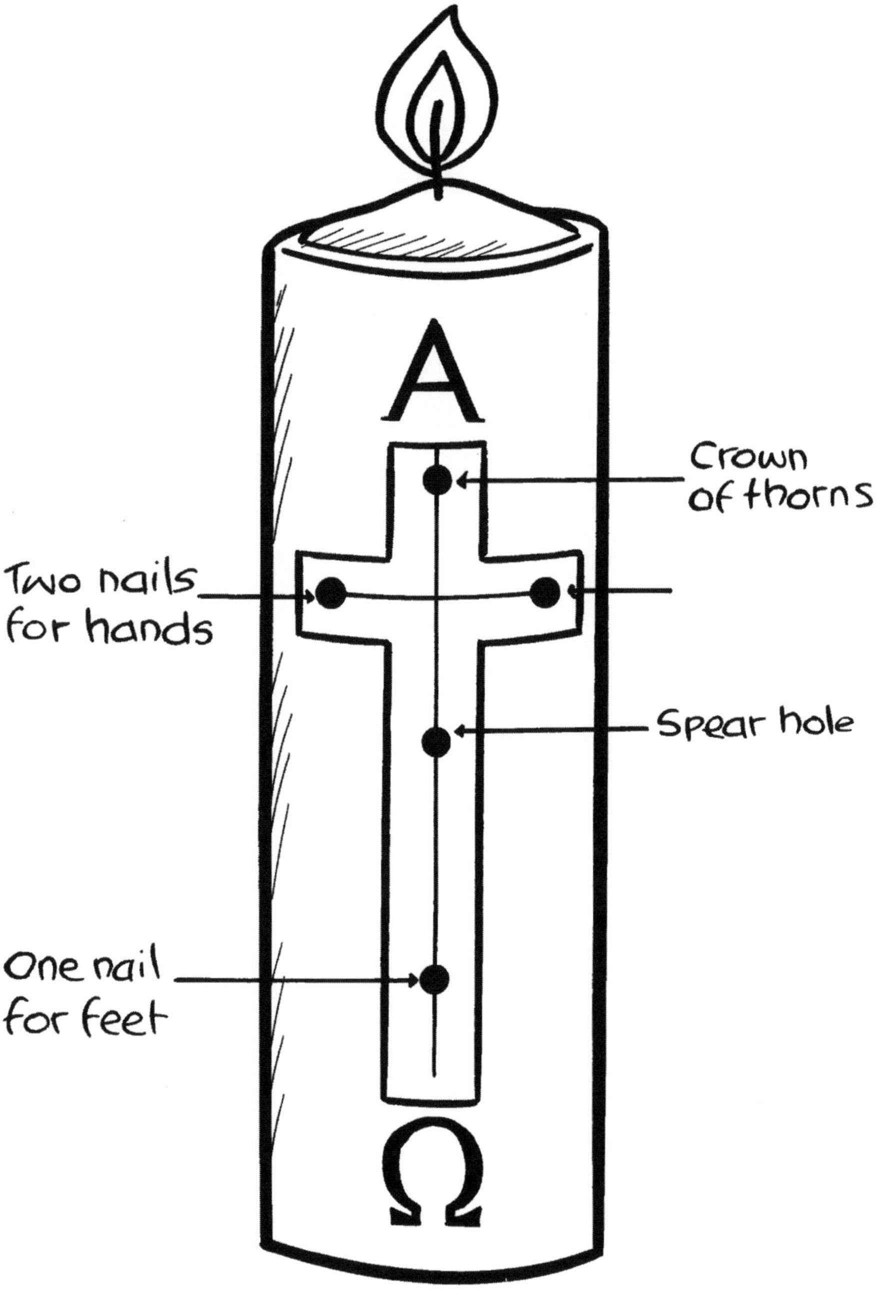
A
Crown
of thorns
Two nails
for hands
Spear hole
One nail
for feet
Ω

Ascension Day

Affirmation of God's presence

Affirmation

Today, we give thanks that our Lord Jesus Christ is risen from the dead and he has ascended into heaven. May he also be in our hearts and may we know that in him earth and heaven are one.

Invitation to worship

As we meet in the grace and goodness of the Father, the Son and the Holy Spirit, let us rejoice in the glory of the ascension and his presence with us.

Alleluia, Christ is risen.
He is risen indeed, Alleluia,

The Lord is here.
His Spirit is with us.

Hymn

Hail the day that sees him rise

Candle-lighting

Prayer

At the lighting of the Easter Candle.
May Christ, risen in glory, scatter the darkness from our hearts and minds and from this world. The light of the risen Christ shine upon us this day and always.

Risen Lord, this day we rejoice in your glorious ascension, may we show in our lives that we know you and that you are with us always. Help us to walk in your ways and do your will that it may be seen that we dwell in you and you are in us. May we be one with you in your kingdom where you live and reign with the Father and the Holy Spirit, one God now and for ever. **Amen.**

Silence

Ministry of the Word

Reading
Acts 1:1–11

Hymn
Alleluia, sing to Jesus

The Gospel
Luke 24:44–53

After the Gospel is announced, but before it is read, sing Alleluias. ('Celtic Alleluia' by Fintan O'Carroll or the Alleluia from 'Seek ye first the kingdom of God')

Repeat the Alleluias at the end the Gospel.

After the Gospel, at the Easter Candle ***(This should replace the intercessions and possibly the sermon.)*** *There is a diagram of a traditional Easter Candle at the end of today's worship. If you want to add the crown of thorns, the nails and the spear hole to the candle before the service you could use five incense grains or drawing pins. Different people could do a section each. You can have of a crown of thorns made from barbed wire or a thorn bush, two nails for the hands, a single nail for the feet, and a spear for the side.*

Affirm
God, you are the beginning and end of all things.
All things were created out of your love and for your love.
You are the Alpha and the Omega: the beginning and the end.
Creator of time and space:
Saviour beyond time and space;
Spirit within time and space.
We worship and adore you.

Withdraw the incense grain (*or the drawing pin*) for the crown of thorns (or touch the top of the candle).

The head that once was crowned with thorns is now crowned with glory.

Show the crown that is to be put on a table for display.

O dearest Lord, thy sacred head
with thorns was pierced for me;
O pour thy blessing on my head
that I may think for thee.

Lord, we remember before you
the troubled in mind,
all who have painful memories,
the depressed and the despairing.
The mentally disturbed.
Lord, keep our minds strong in the knowledge and love of God
and help us to proclaim your presence and love.
Ascended Lord, may our minds ascend to where you are in glory.
Alleluia.
Alleluia.

Withdraw the grains of incense (*or the drawing pin*) for the hands (or touch two places further down the candle).

Show the two nails and place them with the crown of thorns.

O dearest Lord, thy sacred hands
with nails were pierced for me;
O pour thy blessing on my hands
that they may work for thee.

We remember in your presence all whose hands are idle.
We pray for the unemployed and redundant, the handicapped
and all with waning or failing powers.
We remember all who are tempted to misuse
the power that God has given them.

Lord, we are always in your presence,
may we live to your praise and glory.
We are in the hands of God.
Alleluia.
Alleluia.

Withdraw the incense grain (*or the drawing pin*) for the pierced side of Christ (or move further down the candle).

Show the spear and then place it with the crown and the nails.

Time and again the humans break the heart of God. Yet God never ceases to love us.

O dearest Lord, thy sacred heart
with spear was pierced for me;
O pour thy spirit in my heart
that I may live for thee.

God, we remember before you
all who are betrayed in love,
the broken-hearted and the deserted,
the rejected and the lonely.
We thank you for our loved ones and our friends.
Ascended Lord, as you love us with an everlasting love,
help us to love you and show your love in our love for each other.
Alleluia.
Alleluia.

Withdraw the incense grain (*or the drawing pin*) representing the feet (or place your hands near the base of the candle).

Show the nail that held his feet and place it with the other symbols of Christ's death.

He who was firmly fixed is set free. He is let loose on the world.

O dearest Lord, thy sacred feet
with nails were pierced for me;
O pour thy blessing on my feet
that they may follow thee.

Lord, we remember before you
all who are striving for freedom,
all who are held captive.
We ask your blessing upon all
who seek to do your will
and to bring in the glory of your kingly rule.
We rejoice for death is conquered.
We are free.
Christ has won the victory.
Alleluia.
Alleluia.

Extinguish the Easter candle

Place the unlit candle with the other symbols.

The Lord has gone up on high.
Alleluia.
Alleluia.

Hail the day that sees him rise. Alleluia.
See he lifts his hands above. Alleluia.
See he shows the prints of love. Alleluia.
Hark! His gracious lips bestow. Alleluia.
Blessings on his Church below. Alleluia.

Jesus said, 'I am with you always.'
Alleluia.
Alleluia.

'I go to prepare a place for you that where I am you may be also.'
Alleluia.
Alleluia.

Lord, we remember in your presence all who are in the dark, may they come to your love and light and know you as their ascended Lord and friend. We remember all our loved ones departed and rejoice that we are all united in you.
The Lord is here. Alleluia.
Alleluia.
His Spirit is with us. Alleluia.
Alleluia.

Silence

Hymn
The head that once was crowned with thorns

Response

Creed

Confession

Thanksgiving
Praise and thanks to you Lord our God, for in the ascension of our Lord, you have opened to us the way into your kingdom. As the cloud received him from sight it reminded us of the hidden glory, for Christ is ever with us. We thank you for this vision and the promise of your abiding presence. Blessed are you Father, Son and Holy Spirit one God for ever and ever.
Amen.

Collect
Grant, we pray, almighty God,
that as we believe your only begotten Son, our Lord Jesus Christ
to have ascended into the heavens,
so we in heart and mind may also ascend
and with him continually dwell;
who is alive and reigns with you,
in the unity of the Holy Spirit,
one God, now and for ever.
Amen.

Common Worship Collect for Ascension Day

The Lord's Prayer

Silence

Hymn
Rejoice, the Lord is King

Blessing

The risen and ascended King, Christ our Lord,
grant you a glimpse of his glory
and the knowledge that he is with you now and for evermore:
and the blessing of God Almighty,
the Father, the Son and the Holy Spirit
be upon you and remain with you always.
Amen.

The risen and ascended Lord

Begin in the dark. If the room is not dark, close your eyes.

Welcome the light

We give thanks, for in dying Christ has conquered death; in his ascension he has opened to us the way to everlasting life. While he was blessing them, he withdrew from them and was carried up into heaven.

Luke 24:51

As we meet in the love and light of the Father, the Son and the Holy Spirit, let us rejoice in the power of his resurrection and ascension.

Alleluia, Christ is risen.
He is risen indeed, Alleluia.

The Lord is here.
His Spirit is with us.

Candle-lighting

May Christ, risen in glory, scatter the darkness from our hearts and minds and from this world.
The presence of the ascended Christ be with us, this day and always.

Alleluia, Christ is risen.
He is risen indeed, Alleluia.

Light the candle.

Blessed are you, Lord our God,
for you have raised your Son from the darkness of death
to the fullness of life eternal, to your right hand on high.
By his death he has destroyed death;

by his rising to life again he has restored to us eternal life;
by his ascension he has opened for us the gate of glory.
Blessed are you Father, Son and Holy Spirit.

Reading
Luke 24:44–53

Hymn
Hail the day that sees him rise *(first two verses)*

Special intention – in the light of God

As we rejoice in your ascension, O Christ,
we give you thanks for men and women of vision,
for those who have shared the light of their faith with us.
We remember all whose lives are clouded by doubt or despair,
all who walk in darkness.
Lord, be known to those who feel life is dull and empty,
that they may come to know your joy, ascended Lord.

Closing prayer

Ascended Lord, to you be praise and glory.
We come to you in love
and give our hearts to you.
As you are in heaven,
heaven and our hearts are one.
Ascended Lord, to you be praise and glory.

Extinguish candle.

We are Easter people;
alleluia is our song.

Easter 7
The Sunday after the Ascension

Affirmation of God's presence

Affirmation

We celebrate the Ascension of our Lord and think of the disciples afterwards as they waited for the Spirit of God to fill their lives. We make space in our lives for the Holy Spirit of God to come to us and work through us.

Invitation to worship

We place ourselves before the grace of Lord Jesus Christ, the love of God and the fellowship of the Holy Spirit. We are in the presence of God, the Father, the Son and the Holy Spirit.

Alleluia, Christ is risen.
He is risen indeed, Alleluia.

The Lord is here.
His Spirit is with us.

Hymn

The King is among us

Candle-lighting

Have the Easter Candle in the Sanctuary, or a special place, to represent the Ascension.

May Christ, risen and ascended, scatter the darkness from our hearts and minds and from this world. The light of the ascended Christ shine upon us this day and always. Christ wants us to share his mission. Remember:
Christ has no hands but your hands
to do his work today.
Christ has no feet but your feet
to speed men on his way.

Christ has no lips but your lips
to tell men why he died.
Christ has no love but your love
to win men to his side.
Attributed to St Teresa of Avila

Spirit of God, we need your power, we need your strength, if we are to live and work for the kingdom of God. Come Holy Spirit, fill our lives, guide us and enable us to do what you would have us do.

Silence

Ministry of the Word

Old Testament
Ezekiel 36:24–28

Hymn
Come, let us join our cheerful songs

The Gospel
Luke 24:44–55

After the Gospel is announced, but before it is read, sing Alleluias.
('Celtic Alleluia' by Fintan O'Carroll or the Alleluia from 'Seek ye first the kingdom of God')

After the Gospel has been read:

Alleluia, Christ is risen:
He is risen indeed, Alleluia.

We are Easter people;
Alleluia is our song.

Repeat the Alleluias sung before the Gospel.

Sermon

Silence

Hymn
We have a Gospel to proclaim

Response

Creed

Confession

Thanksgiving
God of all, we give you thanks and praise for the glorious Ascension of Christ our Lord. In his death he has triumphed over death. In his rising to life again he has opened to us the way to eternal life. In his glorious Ascension, he who came down has returned to the fullness of his kingdom. He came down for us and now we are raised with him. We praise you for we are ever in your presence and you give your Spirit to us. Lord may we learn to rejoice in the reality that dwells in you and know that you dwell in us. To you be glory and praise for ever, Father, Son and Holy Spirit.

Intercessions
Lord Jesus Christ, risen and ascended,
may our hearts be with you, for then our hearts are in heaven.
We wait upon the gift of the Spirit
that we may be guided and empowered
to do what you would have us do:
that we may be the people you want us to be
and that we may share in your mission of love to the world.
We ask your blessing upon all
who are being baptised or confirmed at this time,
all who are seeking to be ordained,
may we all be Spirit-filled and charismatic people.
Risen and ascended Christ,
king of glory, give us the gift of your Holy Spirit.

Guide us by the power of your Spirit
that the powers of evil may be defeated:
that peace may come to the earth:
that the kingdoms of the world may become your kingdom.
We ask your blessing upon all who strive for unity and peace,
all who care for this world and the people who live upon it.
Risen and ascended Christ,
king of glory, give us the gift of your Holy Spirit.

Fill us with your Holy Spirit, that our hearts may be uplifted:
that our hearts may reflect your glory:
that we may be at home with you in our homes.
We ask your blessing upon our homes and loved ones,
upon the communities to which we belong.
We remember before you all who are struggling
with their relationships and with their lives.
Risen and ascended Christ,
king of glory, give us the gift of your Holy Spirit.

May your Holy Spirit come and refresh and renew us:
that those who are down may be lifted up:
that the downtrodden may arise to a new freedom:
that the ill, those suffering from handicaps or disabilities
may find new hope.
We ask your blessing upon all who use their gifts
to relieve suffering and to bring healing.
Risen and ascended Christ,
king of glory, give us the gift of your Holy Spirit.

Risen and ascended Christ, we remember before you our loved ones departed. May they rejoice in your presence and be renewed and restored in the power of your Spirit. May we all rejoice in your eternal kingdom.
Merciful Father,
accept these prayers for the sake of your Son,
our Saviour Jesus Christ.
Amen.

Collect

O God, the king of glory, you have exalted your only Son Jesus Christ with great triumph to your kingdom in heaven: we beseech you, leave us not comfortless, but send your Holy Spirit to strengthen us and exalt us to the place where our Saviour Christ is gone before, who is alive and reigns with you, in the unity of the Holy Spirit, one God, now and for ever.

Common Worship Collect for the Seventh Sunday after Easter

The Lord's Prayer

Silence

Hymn

Forth in thy name, O Lord, I go

Blessing

Almighty God give you his boundless love:
Christ ascended bring to you the joys of everlasting life:
the power of the Holy Spirit come to you in all that you do:
and the blessing of God Almighty,
the Father, the Son and the Holy Spirit
be upon you and remain with you always.
Amen.

The risen and ascended Christ

Begin in the dark. If the room is not dark, close your eyes.

Welcome the light

We give thanks, for in dying Christ has conquered death; in his ascension he has opened to us the way to everlasting life. As they were watching, he was lifted up, and a cloud took him out of their sight.

Acts 1:9

As we meet in the love and light of the Father, the Son and the Holy Spirit, let us rejoice in the power of his resurrection and ascension.

Alleluia, Christ is risen.
He is risen indeed, Alleluia.

The Lord is here.
His Spirit is with us.

Candle-lighting

May Christ, risen in glory, scatter the darkness from our hearts and minds and from this world.
The presence of the ascended Christ be with us, this day and always.

Alleluia, Christ is risen.
He is risen indeed, Alleluia.

Light the candle.

God of all, we give you thanks and praise for the glorious ascension of Christ our Lord. In his death he has triumphed over death. In his rising to life again he has opened to us the way to eternal life. In his glorious ascension he who came down has returned to the fullness of his kingdom. He came down for us and now we are raised with him. We praise you, for we are ever in your presence and you give your Spirit to us. Lord, may we learn to rejoice in the reality that we dwell in you and know that you dwell in us. To you be glory and praise for ever, Father, Son and Holy Spirit.

Reading

Acts 1:6–11

Hymn

The head that once was crowned with thorns *(first three verses)*

Special intention – in the light of God

Risen and ascended Christ,
may our hearts be with you, for then our hearts are in heaven.
We wait upon the gift of the Spirit
that we may be guided and empowered to do what you would have us do:
that we may be the people you want us to be
and that we may share in your mission of love to the world.
We ask your blessing upon all who are being baptised or confirmed at this time,
all who are seeking to be ordained; may we all be Spirit-filled and charismatic people.
Risen and ascended Christ,
King of glory, give us of your Holy Spirit.

Risen and ascended Christ,
may your Holy Spirit come and refresh and renew us:
that those who are down may be lifted up:
that the downtrodden may arise to a new freedom:
that all ill, those suffering from handicaps or disabilities may find new hope.
We ask your blessing upon all who use their gifts to relieve suffering
and to bring healing.
Risen and ascended Christ,
King of glory, give us of your Holy Spirit.

Closing prayer

Christ, you came down
that we might rise with you.
Christ, you share our humanity
that we may partake of your Divinity.
Christ, you ascended into heaven
that we might be one with you in your kingdom.
Christ, risen and ascended,
may we abide with you for ever.

Extinguish candle.

We are Easter people;
alleluia is our song.

Pentecost

Affirmation of God's presence

Affirmation

For fifty days we have celebrated the resurrection, the victory of our Lord over sin and death. Now we rejoice in the coming of the Spirit upon the disciples. We welcome the Spirit into our lives and we seek to live and work in the power the Spirit gives to us.

Invitation to worship

As we meet in the power and presence of God, Father, Son and Holy Spirit, let us rejoice in gifts the Holy Spirit brings to each of us.

Alleluia, Christ is risen.
He is risen indeed, Alleluia.

The Lord is here.
His Spirit is with us.

Hymn

Come down, O Love divine

Silence

Ministry of the Word

Reading

Acts 2:1–21

Hymn

Spirit of God unseen as the wind

The Gospel

John 14:15–31

After the Gospel is announced, but before it is read, sing Alleluias.
('Celtic Alleluia' by Fintan O'Carroll or the Alleluia from 'Seek ye first the kingdom of God')

Candle-lighting

The Easter Candle should stand in the Sanctuary, or a special place, to represent the Ascension. Have thirteen people light candles from the Easter Candle. Let them say the first sentence together, then a sentence each as they light their candle.

We light these candles for the disciples upon whom the Spirit came at Pentecost.
I light this candle for Peter.
I light this candle for Andrew.
I light this candle for James.
I light this candle for John.
I light this candle for Philip.
I light this candle for Bartholomew.
I light this candle for Thomas.
I light this candle for Matthew.
I light this candle for the other James.
I light this candle for Thaddaeus.
I light this candle for Simon.
I light this candle for Matthias who replaced Judas Iscariot.

I light this special candle for us, for God gives us the gift of his Spirit.
Alleluia, the Lord is here.
His Spirit is with us, Alleluia.

We are Easter people;
Alleluia is our song.

Repeat the Alleluias sung before the Gospel.

Prayer

Breathe in us, Holy Spirit,
that we may think what is holy.
Move in us, Holy Spirit,
that we may do what is holy.
Attract us, Holy Spirit,
that we may love what is holy.
Strengthen us, Holy Spirit,
that we may guard what is holy.
Guard us, Holy Spirit,
that we may keep what is holy.

St Augustine of Hippo 354–430 Adapted

Silence

Sermon

Silence

Hymn

Breathe on me, Breath of God

Response

Creed

Confession

Thanksgiving

Blessed are you, Lord our God, to you be praise and glory for ever. At the beginning of creation your Spirit brought order out of chaos and a world out of your love. In the power of the Spirit you breathed life into the world and all creation rejoiced in your love. We thank you for the gift of life and that your Spirit is with us and within us. We praise you for the gifts the Spirit has given to us and to all peoples, for the talents and abilities that come from the Spirit. As we give you praise, pour your Spirit upon us and set our hearts on fire with love for you, Father, Son and Holy Spirit.
Amen.

Intercessions

Come, Holy Spirit, breath of God, and renew us and inspire us.
Come, Holy Spirit, wind of God, refresh us
and move us to do what is right.
Come, Holy Spirit, fire of God, warm our hearts
and disperse all dullness and coldness.
Come, Holy Spirit, power of God, enable us and help us
to live to your glory.
Come, Holy Spirit, as you did to the disciples,
and fill your Church with your presence and power.
Come, Holy Spirit, on all who seek to preach or minister
or share in your mission to the world.
Holy Spirit, come upon us:
hear us and help us.

Come, Holy Spirit, inspire peoples and nations with your gift of peace: guide and give vision to all artists, musicians and craftspeople: enlighten and direct all research workers, scientists, and conservationists, all who seek to care for the world, its beauty and its environment.
Holy Spirit, come upon us:
hear us and help us.

Come, Holy Spirit, as you filled the house where the disciples were,
fill our homes and our hearts.
Let us know that we dwell in you and you are in us.
We ask your blessing upon all homes
where there is lack of love or respect
and pray that they may find peace and new life in you.
Holy Spirit, come upon us:
hear us and help us.

Come, Holy Spirit, Giver of life, breathe newness into all who are exhausted, weary or without hope. Give of your Spirit to the despondent and the dispirited. We bring before you all who struggle in any way and all who cannot cope on their own. May they know your love and your power. Spirit of God renew, refresh, restore us.
Holy Spirit, come upon us:
hear us and help us.

Come, Holy Spirit, that in your renewing we may know that life is

eternal. To you we commit all our loved ones departed for in you they are filled with newness of life.
Merciful Father,
accept these prayers for the sake of your Son,
our Saviour Jesus Christ.
Amen.

Collect

Lord, you have taught us
that all our doings without love are nothing worth:
send your Holy Spirit
and pour into our hearts that most excellent gift of love,
the true bond of peace and of all virtues,
without which whosoever is counted dead before you.
Grant this for your Son Jesus Christ's sake,
who is alive and reigns with you,
in the unity of the Holy Spirit, one God, now and for ever.
Amen.

Common Worship Collect for Second Sunday after Trinity

The Lord's Prayer

Silence

Hymn

The Spirit lives to set us free

Blessing

The Holy Spirit of God come upon you,
breathe new life into you,
set your hearts on fire with love,
and empower you to live and work to his glory:
and the blessing of God Almighty,
the Father, the Son and the Holy Spirit
be upon you now and for ever more.
Amen.

Holy Spirit, inspire us

Begin in the dark. If the room is not dark, close your eyes.

Welcome the light

We rejoice this day in the coming of the Holy Spirit.

Divided tongues, as of fire, appeared among them, and a tongue rested on each of them. All of them were filled with the Holy Spirit.
Acts 2:3, 4

Candle-lighting

I light this candle for us, for God gives us the gift of his Spirit who came upon the disciples in tongues of flame.
Alleluia, the Lord is here
his Spirit is with us, Alleluia.

We are Easter people;
alleluia is our song.

Light the candle.

Blessed are you, Lord our God; to you be praise and glory for ever.
At the beginning of creation
your Spirit brought order out of chaos
and a world out of your love.
In the power of the Spirit you breathed life into the world
and all creation rejoiced in your love.
We thank you for the gift of life
and that your Spirit is with us and within us.
As we give you praise, pour your Spirit upon us
and set our hearts on fire with love for you,
Father, Son and Holy Spirit.
Amen.

Reading
Acts 2:1–21

Hymn
Come down, O Love divine *(first two verses)*

Special intention – in the light of God

Come, Holy Spirit, breath of God and renew us and inspire us.
Come, Holy Spirit, wind of God, refresh us and move us to do what is right.
Come, Holy Spirit, fire of God, warm our hearts and disperse all dullness and coldness.
Come, Holy Spirit, power of God, enable us and help us to live to your glory.
Come, Holy Spirit, as you did to the disciples.
Holy Spirit, come upon us:
and inspire us.

Come, Holy Spirit, inspire peoples and nations with your gift of peace.
Come, Holy Spirit, guide and give vision to all artists, musicians and craftspeople.
Come, Holy Spirit, enlighten and direct all research workers, scientists, and conservationists.
Come, Holy Spirit, upon all who seek to care for the world, its beauty and its environment.
Holy Spirit, come upon us:
and inspire us.

Come Holy Spirit,
as you filled the house where the disciples were,
fill our homes and our hearts.
Let us know that we dwell in you and that you are in us.
Holy Spirit, come upon us:
and inspire us.

Closing prayer

Breathe in us, Holy Spirit,
that we may think what is holy.
Move in us, Holy Spirit,
that we may do what is holy.
Attract us, Holy Spirit,
that we may love what is holy.
Strengthen us, Holy Spirit,
that we may guard what is holy.
Guard us, Holy Spirit,
that we may keep what is holy.

St Augustine of Hippo 354–430

Extinguish candle.

Trinity

Begin in the dark. If the room is not dark, close your eyes.

Welcome the light

We rejoice today in the threefold nature of our God.
The grace of our Lord Jesus Christ, the love of God, and the communion of the Holy Spirit be with all of you.

2 Corinthians 13:13

Do you believe in God the Creator who made heaven and earth, who made us out of love?
I believe and trust in him.

Do you believe in God the Son, who shared in our humanity, who died and rose again for us?
I believe and trust in him.

Do you believe in God the Holy Spirit, who is the Lord and giver of life and sustains us in our need?
I believe and trust in him.

This is the faith of the whole Church.
I believe and love one God, Father, Son and Holy Spirit.

Candle-lighting

We light this candle as an expression of the love of God for us and that he gives light to our lives.
Jesus Christ is the Light of the World.
A light that no darkness can quench.

Light the candle.

Blessed be God, Father, Son and Holy Spirit,
the Three in One, the holy and wonderful Trinity
bound together in one eternity of love.
Blessed be God, the creator of all things.
Blessed be the Christ, our Saviour and Friend.
Blessed be the Spirit within us, our Guide and Strength.
Blessed be God, for all that he is and all he has done.
Blessed be the One and the Three.
Blessed be God for ever.

Reading
John 16:12–15

Hymn
Father of heaven, whose love profound

Special intention – in the light of God

Father, we give you thanks for your creation, for the beauty and wonder of our world. We ask your blessing upon all who work in caring for the earth and who labour to provide us with our daily needs.
Holy, holy, holy God,
hear us and help us.

Jesus Christ, Son of God, we give thanks for your love revealed in our salvation. May we share with you in the bringing of all people to a greater freedom. We ask your blessing upon all who are caring for the ill and the hungry of our world.
Holy, holy, holy God,
hear us and help us.

Holy Spirit of God, may we know your presence with us and within us. We give thanks for the talents and the abilities you give to us. We pray for all scientists and research workers; for all artists and craftspeople.
Holy, holy, holy God,
hear us and help us.

Closing prayer

I live today in the power of the Father.
I live today in the love of the Saviour.
I live today in the light of the Spirit.
I live today in newness of life.
I live today in freshness and renewal.
I live today in time and for eternity.
I live today in the grace and goodness of the Holy Trinity.

Extinguish candle.

Transfiguration

Begin in the dark. If the room is not dark, close your eyes.

Welcome the light

In their spending time alone with Jesus on the mountain, Peter, James and John became aware of his glory.

The Word became flesh and lived among us, and we have seen his glory, the glory as of a father's only son, full of grace and truth.

John 1:14

Candle-lighting

We light this candle as an expression of the glory of God, revealed in the face of Jesus Christ; asking that our lives may burn with his glory.
Jesus Christ is the Light of the World.
A light that no darkness can quench.

Light the candle.

Blessed are you, Lord our God,
for you have revealed yourself through Moses and the prophets.
you have made yourself known to us through your saints,
but above all you show us your glory in the face of our Lord
Jesus Christ.
As we open our lives to his glory may we reflect it in all the world.
Blessed are you, Father, Son and Holy Spirit.

Reading

Luke 9:28–36

Hymn

Christ, whose glory fills the skies

Special intention – in the light of God

Lord, change us and we shall be changed.
Transform our homes into places of your glory.
Transform our lives to reveal your presence.
Transform our minds to know your peace.
Transform our hearts to abide in your love.
May we know you are always with our loved ones and with us.
God, in your goodness,
grant us a glimpse of your glory.

Lord, change us and we shall be changed.
Transform our darkness with your light.
Transform our weakness with your strength.
Transform our fear by your protection.
Transform our loneliness by your presence.
Transform us that we may reflect your glory.
God, in your goodness,
grant us a glimpse of your glory.

Closing prayer

Awaken us to your glory:
dispel the darkness of night;
destroy the heaviness of heart;
cure the blindness of sight;
heal the deafness of ears;
open the mouth that is dumb;
restore a gentleness of touch;
encourage a sense of adventure;
bring us an awareness of you.
Awaken us to your glory.

Extinguish candle.

All Saints

Begin in the dark. If the room is not dark, close your eyes.

Welcome the light

Today we rejoice in the Communion of Saints and give thanks to God for all who have witnessed to his love and power.

The holy ones of the Most High shall receive the kingdom and possess the kingdom for ever – for ever and ever.

Daniel 7:18

Candle-lighting

As we light the candle, we rejoice in the fellowship of the saints in light.

Jesus Christ is the Light of the World.
A light that no darkness can quench.

Light the candle.

Blessed are you, Lord our God,
for you have called us to share in the fellowship of all your saints.
Grant that in the darkness that is about us
we may be guided by their example
and so serve you in love and in peace.
Blessed are you, Father, Son and Holy Spirit.

Reading

1 Corinthians 1:26–31

Hymn

For all the saints *(first three verses)*

Special intention – in the light of God

Rejoicing in the fellowship of all the saints, we pray to the Lord:
Lord, make us to be numbered with your saints,
in your eternal glory.

Blessed God, we remember before you
all who have set us an example by their grace and goodness.
We ask your blessing upon our homes and families.
We pray for all who are suffering from broken relationships and all who feel lonely.
Lord, make us to be numbered with your saints,
in your eternal glory.

Blessed God, we remember before you
all who have suffered persecution for their faith.
We ask you to bless those who strive against injustice and evil.
We pray for all who suffer from tyranny or oppression.
Lord, make us to be numbered with your saints,
in your eternal glory.

Closing prayer

Dearest Lord, teach me to be generous;
teach me to serve you as you deserve;
to give and not to count the cost,
to fight and not to heed the wounds,
to toil and not to seek for rest,
to labour and not to seek a reward,
save that of knowing that I do your will.
Ignatius Loyola 1491–1556

Extinguish candle.

Remembrance Day

Affirmation of God's presence

Affirmation

We are in the presence of God who created the world out of his love and made us in his image. He has allowed us the freedom to choose, to acknowledge him and the wholeness of his world or through selfishness and sin to mar his creation and to seek to control and have power over others. We remember today all who have given their lives in the service of others, all who have suffered and are suffering through war. We ask God's help to guide us into the ways of justice and peace.

God, Father, Son and Holy Spirit,
we are in your presence,
your peace and your power.
Amen.

God of love and peace, we come,
with all who seek to keep this day,
to show our gratitude for all who have given their lives
that we may live in freedom.
We remember all who have seen war as a necessary evil,
and those who believe that no one should take up arms.
We think of those who fought
and gave their lives out of duty; those who refused to fight
through conscientious objection
and who suffered for their belief.
We remember all who died,
and all returned injured or scarred in body, mind or spirit.
We remember the countless made homeless and all who are left
sorrowing and alone.
We ask your blessing upon all
who seek to restore shattered communities and broken lives.

Hymn

O God, our help in ages past

Act of penitence

Let us remember before God, sins of division and conflict in our own lives, our desire to triumph over others . . .
God of peace,
lead us in the ways of peace.

Prince of Peace,
lead us in the ways of peace.

Spirit Giver of peace,
lead us in the ways of peace.

By your self-offering upon the cross
Lord, inspire us.

By your willingness to die for us
Lord, inspire us.

By your love and your care for all,
Lord, inspire us.

For all our attempts to control and triumph over others
Lord, forgive us.

For our trust in might and in violence
Lord, forgive us.

For our hidden hatred and prejudices
Lord, forgive us.

For turning a blind eye to evil
Lord, forgive us.

For our standing by whilst others suffer
Lord, forgive us.

For our silence when peace is challenged
Lord, forgive us.

Let us confess in silence our sins and failings towards unity and community, towards each other and towards God.

A short silence for reflection

Holy God,
Holy and strong,
Holy and immortal,
have mercy upon us.

Or

Most merciful God
Father of our Lord Jesus Christ,
we confess that we have sinned
in thought, word and deed.
We have not loved you with our whole heart.
We have not loved our neighbour as ourselves.
In your mercy, forgive what we have been,
help us to amend what we are,
and direct what we shall be;
that we may do justly,
love mercy,
and walk humbly with you our God.
Amen

From Common Worship

Almighty God, who has promised to forgive all who truly repent,
grant us forgiveness and absolution from all our sins,
time to amend our lives,
peace in all our dealings,
and love in our hearts;
through Jesus Christ our Lord.
Amen.

Reading

John 15:9–17 or Matthew 5:1–12

Waste

Waste of Muscle, waste of Brain,
Waste of Patience, waste of Pain,
Waste of Manhood, waste of Health,
Waste of Beauty, waste of Wealth,
Waste of Blood and waste of Tears,
Waste of Youth's most precious years,
Waste of ways the Saints have trod,
Waste of Glory, waste of God –
War!

G. A. Studdert Kennedy

Hymn

Thy kingdom come, O God

Sermon

Intercessions

God you created us all in you own image, help us to discern your presence in all your children that we may work for unity and peace. Let there be peace in our hearts, peace in our relationships and peace in all our dealings. May our lives and our communities work for peace and live in peace. Bless all leaders and rulers that they may have the wisdom and courage to know and to stand for justice and what is right.
Lord, hear us:
mercifully hear us.

We ask you to guide by your Spirit all who work for unity, all who work to improve and develop relationships between people of different races, creeds and colour. Bless all who work to relieve poverty, to break down prejudice, all who seek to protect and help the persecuted. We remember all who are involved in war or conflict at this time.
Lord, hear us:
mercifully hear us.

O Lord, give courage and hope to all who have suffered through war and all who still suffer. We ask your blessing upon all who have lost faith in you or in humankind, all who are distressed and disturbed. We remember all who have lost loved ones, homes or possessions. We remember with sorrow the destructiveness of all warfare. We ask your blessing upon all who gave their lives.
Lord, hear us:
mercifully hear us.

O God, the author of peace
and lover of concord,
to know you is eternal life,
to serve you is perfect freedom.
Defend us your servants
from all assaults of our enemies;
that we surely trusting in your defence,
may not fear the power of any adversaries;
through Jesus Christ our Lord.
Amen.

Common Worship, Morning Prayer

Hymn
For the healing of the nations

Or

God! As with silent hearts we bring to mind
how hate and war diminish humankind,
we pause, and seek in worship to increase
our knowledge of the things that make for peace.

Hallow our will as humbly we recall
the lives of those who gave and give their all.
We thank you, Lord, for women, children, men
who seek to serve in love, today as then.

Give us deep faith to comfort those who mourn,
high hope to share with all the newly born,
strong love in our pursuit of human worth;
'lest we forget' the future of this earth.

So, Prince of Peace, disarm our trust in power,
teach us to coax the plant of peace to flower.
May we, impassioned by your living Word,
remember forward to a world restored.
Fred Kaan Tune: Stoner Hill

Act of remembrance

Let us remember before God and commend to his love men and women of all nations who have died as a result of tyranny or war; those who we have known and whose memories we treasure, [especially those whose names are engraved here].
If the names at the War Memorial are to be read out this is where to do it.

We remember all who have given their lives in the service of humankind, all who have given their lives for freedom, justice and the hope of peace.

They shall not grow old as we that are left grow old;
age shall not weary them nor the years condemn.
At the going down of the sun
and in the morning we will remember them.
We will remember them.

The Last Post may be sounded.

If the Last Post and Reveille are to be used, it is good to explain at the beginning of the Act of Remembrance their meaning. The Last Post is for the end of the day, for lights going out and so for mortality and death and the fact we do not have ultimate control. It is played for all who have died. The Silence is for us to pray for all who have suffered, who continue to suffer and for all who have died. The Reveille is the call to awake, to newness of life, it is a symbol of hope, of joy, of the resurrection and that our lives are in the hand of God.

THE SILENCE *Usually for two minutes*

Remember before God all the troubled places of the world;
and pray for its peace.
Remember those who have suffered as the result of war
and all who are persecuted for objecting to war.
Ask God's blessing upon all who have died and those who are bereaved.

The Reveille may be sounded.

Almighty and most loving God, you give life and life eternal to all who seek to show your love and to bring in your peace. We ask your blessing upon all whom we remember this day. In you, O God, may they know the peace that passes all understanding and the love that knows no end: through him who lived and died for us Jesus Christ our Lord.
Amen.

Act of commitment

To remember the past is to commit ourselves to the future.
To remember war is to commit ourselves to peace.
To remember violence and tyranny is to commit ourselves to love.
Let us promise to strive for peace in our world starting in our hearts and in our homes.
Let us promise to build peace into our community, our neighbourhood,
our country and our world.

Say together:

Lord, make us instruments of your peace.
Where there is hatred, let us sow love;
where there is injury, let us bring forgiveness;
where there is doubt, let us offer faith;
where there is darkness, let us bring light;
where there is despair, let us offer hope;
and where there is sadness, let us bring joy.
For it is in giving that we receive;
it is in forgiving that we are forgiven;
and in dying that we are born again to eternal life.

The Prayer of St Francis

The Lord's Prayer.

Hymn
I the Lord of sea and sky *or* Peace is flowing like a river

The blessing

The Lord lead you from death to life,
from falsehood to truth.
Lead you from despair to hope,
from fear to trust.
Lead you from hatred to love,
from war to peace.
Let peace of God fill your hearts, your world, your universe:
and the blessing of God Almighty,
the Father, the Son and Holy Spirit
be upon you and your loved ones now and always.
Amen.

Other Occasions

Birth

Begin in the dark. If the room is not dark, close your eyes.

Welcome the light

Behold, children are a heritage from the Lord, the fruit of the womb is a reward.

Psalm 127:3 NKJV

Holy God, we give you thanks for the gift of life and especially the life of this child who is given to us. As you created us all out of love, may we pour our love on this child who is yours and ours.

Candle-lighting

As we light this candle, we give thanks to God for life in his light.
Jesus Christ is the Light of the World.
A light that no darkness can quench.

Light the candle.

Blessed are you, Lord our God,
for you give life and love to all of your creatures.
We rejoice in the gift of our lives
and in the life of this newborn child.
We lift *her* up to you and ask your blessing upon *her*.
Blessed are you, Father, Son and Holy Spirit.

Reading

Luke 2:8–20

Hymn

For the beauty of the earth *(first three verses)*

Special intention – in the light of God

Praise, glory and thanksgiving are yours, O Lord.
you are the giver of life and life eternal.
you have created us, and give your Spirit to us.
Be known to be with *name*
in *her* joys and in *her* sorrows,
in sickness and in health,
in *her* successes and in *her* failures,
in *her* home and in *her* travels.
Bless *her* with your love now and for evermore.

Closing prayer

God, we give you thanks and praise for life.
We rejoice in the gift of this child to us.
Holy Father, be *her* strength.
Lord Jesus, be *her* protector.
Holy Spirit, be *her* guide.
Father, Son and Holy Spirit, be always with *her*,
and keep *her* in your peace.

Extinguish candle.

Journeying

Begin in the dark. If the room is not dark, close your eyes.

Welcome the light

We rejoice in the presence of God and light a candle to remind us that God goes with us wherever we travel.

God said: 'My presence will go with you, and I will give you rest.'
Exodus 33:14

Candle-lighting

Jesus Christ is the Light of the World.
A light that no darkness can quench.

Light the candle.

Blessed are you, Lord our God, for you have created all things and formed us in your own image. Wherever we travel we can see your works and know that you are with us. In everyone we meet we have the opportunity of seeing your image and encountering your presence. In all our journeying you are there, ever present, ready to guide, support and direct us. Blessed are you, Father, Son and Holy Spirit.

Readings
Psalm 139:1–18

Hymn
One more step along the world I go

The path of right
My walk this day with God,
my walk this day with Christ,
my walk this day with Spirit,
the Threefold all kindly:
Ho! ho! ho! the Threefold all kindly.

My shielding this day from ill,
my shielding this night from harm,
ho! ho! both my soul and my body,
be by Father, by Son, by Holy Spirit.
Be the Father shielding me,
be the Son shielding me,
be the Spirit shielding me,
as Three and as One:
Ho! ho! ho! as Three and as One.

Carmina Gadelica III:49

Special intention – in the light of God

God, you seek us when we hide:
to you we sing our songs of praise.

God, you meet us when we seek:
to you we sing our songs of praise.

God, you called Abram to walk into the unknown:
to you we sing our songs of praise.

God, you led Moses through the desert:
to you we sing our songs of praise.

God, you encouraged Joshua to 'go forward':
to you we sing our songs of praise.

God, you travel with all your people:
to you we sing our songs of praise.

We ask your blessing upon people who are on the move.
We remember those who are leaving home or setting up a new home.
We bring before you the homeless, the refugees and all displaced persons.
We remember all who are setting off for new places of work, or to do new projects.
We remember all who are travelling in places of danger,
all who are weary, all who have lost their way, all who are in the dark.

God, companion of all, make yourself known to each in their journey that their 'hearts may burn within them' with your love.

Closing prayer

May the strength of God pilot us.
May the power of God preserve us.
May the wisdom of God instruct us.
May the hand of God protect us.
May the way of God direct us.
May the shield of God defend us.
May the host of God guard us.
Attributed to St Patrick

Extinguish candle.

Loved ones leaving

Begin in the dark. If the room is not dark, close your eyes.

Welcome the light

We rejoice in our love for each other and know that wherever we go we are in the love of God.

Jesus said: 'Remember I am with you always, to the end of the age.'
Matthew 28:20

Candle-lighting

Jesus Christ is the Light of the World.
A light that no darkness can quench.

Light the candle.

Blessed are you, Lord our God,
for you created us out of love and for your love.
You have commanded that we love one another
as you have loved us.
Grant that, as we grow in love,
we may grow in our awareness of you
and of your great love for us.
Blessed are you, Father, Son and Holy Spirit.

Reading
1 John 4:7–12

Hymn
God be with you till we meet again

Special intention – in the light of God

God of love, we remember before you
all who are separated from loved ones

through illness, war, or occupation.
God of love,
be with us.

God of love, we bring before you
all who are struggling with their relationships,
all who are lonely and all who feel deserted.
God of love,
be with us.

God of love, we give you thanks for our home,
for each of our loved ones,
and all who are dear to us.
God of love,
be with us.

God of love, ask your blessing on *name*,
as *she* leaves for *place or reason*.
May *she* know *she* is enfolded in your love
and is ever under your protection.
God of love,
be with us.

Closing prayer

The love of God go with you.
The peace of God be upon you.
God go behind you to protect you.
God go before you to guide you.
God be there to welcome you.
God be on your left to defend you.
God be on your right to strengthen you.
God be beneath you to uphold you.
God be above you to raise you up.
God be within you and about you,
until we meet again.

Extinguish candle.

In times of darkness

Begin in the dark. If the room is not dark, close your eyes.

Welcome the light

The people who walked in darkness have seen a great light; they who lived in a land of deep darkness, on them the light has shined.

Isaiah 9:2

Come, Lord of Life,
come with your light.
Come, enter the darkness of my life.
Come, that I may walk in the light of your Love.
Come, that I may walk in the newness of this day.

Candle-lighting

In our darkness we are not alone; the Lord of Light is ever present.
Jesus Christ is the Light of the World.
A light that no darkness can extinguish.

Light the candle.

Reading

Isaiah 4:1–3 or Psalm 23

Hymn

Lead us, heavenly Father, lead us

Special intention – in the light of God

Holy God, holy and Strong One, in my emptiness I come to be filled by you.
Lord, you are my light and my salvation.

Holy God, holy and Strong One, in my darkness I come to your light.
Lord, you are my light and my salvation.

Holy God, holy and Strong One, in my troubles I come to your love.
Lord, you are my light and my salvation.

Holy God, holy and Strong One, in my illness I come for your healing.
Lord, you are my light and my salvation.

Holy God, holy and Strong One, in my need I come to your salvation.
Lord, you are my light and my salvation.

Lord, you know my needs before I ask
and are always more ready to give than I desire or deserve.
I come to rest in the love of your presence.
I come for renewal and refreshment.
I come for the fullness of life-eternal.
Amen.

Closing prayer

Lord, you love me
with an everlasting love.
When I lose sight of you,
your eye is upon me.
When I lose hold on you,
you enfold me in your love.
When I am in the dark,
the light of your presence is with me.
Lord, you love me
with an everlasting love.
Light incomprehensible, of dazzling brightness,
surround me with the radiance of your glory.

Extinguish candle.

A light for someone

Begin in the dark. If the room is not dark, close your eyes.

Welcome the light

Today we light a candle for *name* that *he* may know the light and love of God.

Walk while you have the light, so that the darkness will not overtake you. If you walk in the darkness, you do not know where you are going. While you have the light, believe in the light, so that you may become children of light.

John 12:35, 36

Candle-lighting

Jesus Christ is the Light of the World.
A light that no darkness can quench.

Light the candle.

Blessed are you, Lord our God, for you love us with an everlasting love. you care for all of your creation and you are with us always. May your love and your presence be known to *name* that *he* may walk in your light and live in your peace. Blessed are you, Father, Son and Holy Spirit.

Name,
may the blessing of light be upon you,
light about you,
light within you.
May the Christ light shine upon you,
warm your heart
and shine from your eyes.

Reading

Psalm 121

Hymn
Thou, whose almighty word

Special intention – in the light of God

God of light, we ask you to guide,
to enlighten,
to fill with your radiance
our loved one this day.
God of love, we ask you to embrace,
to be with,
to fill with your love
our loved one this day.
God of peace, we ask you to calm,
to give rest to,
to support,
our loved one this day.

Closing prayer

Lord, fill *name*:
fill *him* with your peace.
Fill *him* with your presence.
Lord, fill *name*:
fill *him* with your grace.
Fill *him* with your goodness.
Lord, fill *name*:
fill *him* with your love.
Fill *him* with your light.

Extinguish candle, or, if this is a votive candle in a safe place, you may choose to say far fewer words and let the candle burn as your prayer. God knows our needs. Leave the candle burning, knowing he hears you.

For the departed

This service can be used on All Souls' Day, 2 November.

Begin in the dark. If the room is not dark, close your eyes.

Welcome the light

We rejoice this day that in Christ Jesus light has conquered darkness and life has triumphed over death.

Jesus said: 'I am the resurrection and the life. Those who believe in me, though they die, will live, and everyone who lives and believes in me will never die.'

John 11:25, 26

Candle-lighting

Jesus Christ is the Light of the World.
A light no darkness can quench.

Light the candle.

Blessed be the Lord, the God of Israel,
for he has looked favourably on his people and redeemed them.
He has raised up a mighty saviour for us
In the house of his servant David.
By the tender compassion of our God,
the dawn from on high will break upon us,
to shine on those who sit in darkness and the shadow of death:
to guide our feet into the way of peace.

From the Song of Zechariah, Luke 1:68, 69, 78, 79

Reading
1 Corinthians 15:35–58

Give rest, O Christ, to thy servant with thy saints:
where sorrow and pain are no more;
neither sighing but life everlasting.
Thou only art immortal, the creator and maker of man:
and we are mortal formed from the dust of the earth,
and unto earth shall we return:
for so thou didst ordain,
when thou created me saying:
'Dust thou art and unto dust shalt thou return.'
All we go down to the dust;
and weeping o'er the grave we make our song:
Alleluia, alleluia, alleluia.
Give rest, O Christ, to thy servant with thy saints:
where sorrow and pain are no more;
neither sighing but life everlasting.

Russian Kontakion for the Dead

Special intention – in the light of God

O God, Creator and Giver of life and life eternal,
have mercy upon us.

O Christ, triumphing over death, and our Redeemer,
have mercy upon us.

O Holy Spirit, Breath of Life, and Restorer,
have mercy upon us.

O Holy and Blessed Trinity
have mercy upon us.

Give rest, O Lord, to your servant with your saints:
Lord, hear us.

Grant that *she* may be where sorrow and sighing are no more:
Lord, hear us.

That *she* may come to see you and know you:
Lord, hear us.

That *she* may love you and serve you:
Lord, hear us.

That *she* may enjoy the presence in the fullness of your kingdom:
Lord, hear us.

That *she* may abide with you for ever:
Lord, hear us.

That we may see that our end is no end:
Lord, hear us.

That we may know that, in you, life is eternal
Lord, hear us.

Blessed are you, Lord our God,
for with you are the resurrection and the life:
with you are the rest and peace of our loved ones departed:
in you is our hope and trust:
blessed are you, Father, Son and Holy Spirit
for ever and ever.
Amen.

Closing prayer

We give them back to you, dear Lord, who gave them to us. You did not lose them in giving, so we have not lost them by their return. What you gave you take not away, O Lover of Souls; for what is yours is ours also if we are yours. Your Son has taught us that life is eternal and love is immortal, and death is only an horizon, and an horizon is nothing save the limit of our sight. Lift us up, strong Son of God, that we may see further; cleanse our eyes that we may see more clearly; and draw us closer to yourself that we may know ourselves to be nearer to our loved ones who are with thee. And while thou dost prepare for us, prepare us also for that happy place that, where they are and you are, we too may be for evermore, O dear Lord of life and death.

William Penn 1644–1718

May we live as those who believe in
the love and the presence of God;
the forgiveness of sins;
that, in Christ, life is eternal;
and the blessing of God Almighty, the Father, the Son and the Holy Spirit be upon us and upon our loved ones departed, now and for evermore.
Amen.

Extinguish candle.

Acknowledgements

The publishers wish to thank all those who have given their permission to reproduce copyright material in this publication.

Every effort has been made to trace the owners of copyright material and we hope that no copyright has been infringed. Pardon is sought and apology made if the contrary be the case, and a correction will be made in any reprint of this book.

The Church of Englandís adapted form of the *Revised Common Lectionary*, published as the Principal Service Lectionary in *Common Worship: Services and Prayers for the Church of England*, the Second and Third Service Lectionaries and the *Common Worship* Calendar, also published in the same publication are copyright © The Archbishopsí Council of the Church of England, 1995, 1997. Collects and Psalms from the *Common Worship: Services and Prayers for the Church of England* are copyright © The Archbishopsí Council 2000. *Common Worship: Times and Seasons is Times and Seasons* is copyright © The Archbishops' Council 2006. *The Alternate Service Book for the Church of England* copyright © The Archbishops' Council 1980. Material from these works is reproduced with permission.

Text: *For the healing of the nations* by Fred Kaan is copyright © 1968 Stainer & Bell Ltd.

A New Zealand Prayer Book (1989) – Copyright © The Anglican Church in Aotearoa, New Zealand, Polynesia.

The Estate of Reinhold Niebuhr.

Alexander Carmichael, *Carmina Gadelica*, Volume III, Scottish Academic Press, Edinburgh and London 1976.

Russian Kontakion for the Dead, trans. W. J. Burbeck 1869–1916.